Peace in Hope

Dedication

The God of Peace who has brought all things to light is the same God who raised Jesus from the dead. Our God who dwells in us and through us desires our peace in His eternal hope to be our every waking emotion. He keeps us in perfect peace whose mind is stayed on Him. Every word I have ever written has been for the glory of God Almighty. To Him who sits on the Throne be blessing and honor and glory forever.

Peace in Hope
Reflections of God Moments Book 14
copyright © 2025

All Scripture quotations are taken from The Message, copyright © 1993, 2002, 2018 by Eugene H. Peterson. Used by permission of NavPress. All rights reserved. Represented by Tyndale House Publishers.

Scripture taken from the New King James Version®. Copyright © 1982 by Thomas Nelson. Used by permission. All rights reserved.

Written by: Donesa Walker
Design by: Will Baten
Edited by: Kelley Inderman

How blessed the reader! How blessed the hearers and keepers of these oracle words, all the words written in this book! Time is just about up. Revelation 1:3

What is it that brings you peace?

Where do we find "Blessed Peace"?

Key thought for today:

Blessed Peace!

Blessing is what we all want along with peace. No one wants to stress or be at angst. No one wants to struggle or be constantly attacked. Yet, in here lies a promise of blessed peace and so few indulge because it takes work. When I think of the things I picture that bring me peace, I put them together in this photo. I love the sounds of the ocean, the beauty of the sunset and the fragrance of the rose along with the kiss of the waves along my ankles as I hear the constant ebb and flow of the water pushing against the shore. This to me is tranquility. Now, I don't like heat. I don't like to swim. I don't like thorns and I don't like fishy smells or crowds. This photo isn't reality. It is a dream of a perfect place of peace. John writes from a place of reality as he has been tortured and now abandoned on an island to endure. He has gone through much for the sake of the gospel and yet God chose him as a vessel of revealing the truth. As he opens the book of Revelation, he opens with a promise of blessing from the reading. How blessed the readers, the hearers and the keepers of this Word. Time is almost out. The time is running through the hour-glass as the waves push against the shore. The peace and blessings come from the knowing not the knowledge. Knowledge of what the times ahead hold doesn't bring peace because that isn't what the end is about. Blessed peace comes from the knowing of who He is. You see, I can take a picture of my roses and overlay them on a photo of a sunset beach. I can even take roses with me to take such a photo. The peace isn't in the picture nor the exact location. The peace is in the knowing. If someone asked me my favorite place, I wouldn't say the beach. If someone asked me my favorite flower, I wouldn't say a rose. These together are a picture of what peace represents in my mind and my senses but only in the knowing can this be understood. Blessed peace isn't knowledge of a time, place, thing or situation. Blessed peace is in the knowing His words are real, forever, unwavering and eternal. Blessed peace comes not from safety or even a happy place in our minds but from confidence in Him, in who He is and always will be. Blessed peace comes from reading, hearing and keeping His promises for that is how to know God. A rose cannot be opened by any other means except the unfolding of nature just as a wave cannot be controlled by any means except the voice of God. The Revelation of God is about the Blessed Hope of Peace. Time is of essence.

I, John, am writing this to the seven churches in Asia province: All the best to you from The God Who Is, The God Who Was, and The God About to Arrive, and from the Seven Spirits assembled before his throne, and from Jesus Christ— Loyal Witness, Firstborn from the dead, Ruler of all earthly kings. Glory and strength to Christ, who loves us, who blood-washed our sins from our lives, Who made us a Kingdom, Priests for his Father, forever—and yes, he's on his way! Riding the clouds, he'll be seen by every eye, those who mocked and killed him will see him, People from all nations and all times will tear their clothes in lament. Oh, Yes. - Revelation 1: 4-7

Do you have a vision of His returning? What does it look like?

What is the significance of the many names Paul used to refer to Jesus?

Key thought for today:

Cloud Riding!

There are lots of reasons that I love the aurora and the colors in the sky, but the coolest thing about it is I see it as a party in the Heavens. The beauty of the lights is phenomenal and seen differently in every area of the world but it makes it no less fascinating! As John was writing down his revelations to the seven churches, he referenced Jesus with many names and stated that He will ride the clouds, seen by every eye. That is what I see in these lights. I see the glory of God, this Loyal Witness, this God about to Arrive, riding the clouds and throwing out sparks. I know science describes it as magnetic pulses and storms but my mind sees this Firstborn from the dead having a celebration, cloud riding! I picture this Jesus who blood washed our sins, enjoying Himself and celebrating as another soul is added to the Kingdom or as one joins Him in Heaven. He made us Kingdom Priests so that we can have peace in certainty that He is and does as He says. I especially love that as John sees this cloud riding vision, he states that people from all nations and all times will see Him, every eye, those who mocked and killed Him and it makes me think of the great times ahead. This external hope brings the Peace Speaker into our time and us into His presence. Glory and Strength to Christ who is on His way riding the clouds of Glory! He is the God Who Is, the God who Was and the God About to Arrive because He is the God of all places and times. Many movies have been made about time travel and scientific inquiry made into dimensions and the possibilities of times co-existing. There is an innate fascination with time because it is one of the things we have no way to encompass. Recently time change happened as we set clocks, forward and backwards to accommodate a schedule of time change. This affects our bodies in a huge way as it messes with our internal clocks we habitually set but it doesn't mess with God. He is the God of all times. Time Zones don't affect Him. He isn't affected by our clocks, calendars nor schedules. His time is perfect. He defines the time of His return as no man knows the day/hour. When I first read that, I read it as no one knows when He is returning but now I understand it means so much more. Our times and calendars have us so willy nilly that we honestly don't truly know the day/time. I work with lots of clients who struggle in the area of memory and it is fascinating to me that time and scheduling fades in importance as things of this life fade. This modicum of control slips. This false sense of security we use to manage our time becomes less important. When we turn our eyes on Jesus to look Him full in the face, to understand this cloud rider is the King of Glory, then we understand that time has no priority over Him. Our urgency and must do right now fades into a place and time of peace. Time, the one thing we want to control but cannot ever recapture. The minute we waste is the minute we no longer have. Time, the cloud rider says, is all relative to who He is alone. Time is precious to us because we cannot harness nor control it, buy it nor sell it and yet so often we waste it on things that steal our peace rather than stopping the clock of life's demands to celebrate the Peace Speaker. Time to cloud ride with our Savior. Time to put away the schedules and demands to ride the wings of peace with the One who is and was and always will be as He arrives in all times, forever! Riding the peace clouds, oh yes!

Whenever, though, they turn to face God as Moses did, God removes the veil and there they are—face-to-face! They suddenly recognize that God is a living, personal presence, not a piece of chiseled stone. And when God is personally present, a living Spirit, that old, constricting legislation is recognized as obsolete. We're free of it! All of us! Nothing between us and God, our faces shining with the brightness of his face. And so we are transfigured much like the Messiah, our lives gradually becoming brighter and more beautiful as God enters our lives and we become like him. - 2 Chorinthians 3: 16-18

Are you taking full advantage of the freedom we have to be face to face with God?

How does this intimacy affect your daily life?

Key thought for today:

Face to Face!

One of my favorite moments growing up was watching the groom lift the veil on his bride. Rarely does a bride use a veil anymore but it has such a beautiful message if we understand its meaning. Historically a veil was a shield between the world and the person as a signal of a door. Intimacy between two people is only had when the veil is removed. Jacob was tricked into marrying the sister of the woman he loved because of the veil hiding who she was until after the marriage. The removal of the veil from God's face means that He is removing the stance of a go between from us. We no longer have to go through a priest because Jesus became our High Priest and when the veil was rent at His crucifixion, it was the severance of the old covenant. The old covenant required confession of sin to a priest and blood sacrifice on an altar to take away sin but when Jesus fulfilled the old covenant with His sacrifice, the old covenant no longer applied and the new covenant met all. This doesn't mean there is not important information and purpose to the Old Testament in scripture. In fact it elevates it because it was the law fulfilled by Jesus. When Moses faced God, a veil had to be put over his face because he glowed so much. God removes this veil in revealing Himself as a personal God through The Word fulfilled and The Holy Spirit sent to interpret and reveal-lift the veil-of understanding of The Word. God then goes from being only perceived as a Judge to suddenly a place of intimacy like a Lover of our souls. Instead of being the God who was only, He becomes the God who is and always will be. I will never forget the moment that veil was lifted for me. I will always remember that place of intimacy where I first knew God as the lover of my soul rather than only the parental authenticity who judged me-the chiseled stone of commands. When God becomes intimately connected, personally present, a living Spirit that you feel and breathe and stretch in confidence in, there is no greater feeling of peace and freedom. Nothing between. Face to face. Our lives transformed and transfigured, gradually becoming brighter and more beautiful as intimacy with Him suffuses our lives. The closer we draw to Him, the more like Him we become and then we truly see Him as He is. The veil. The secret. The wall. The closed access. All of it has been removed. God removes it. Not any man could do so but God in the flesh of His son, Jesus fulfilled the covenant and rent that veil forever. This personally present, living Spirit is not bound by constraints of law as He made it all obsolete by fulfillment. We walk in freedom and intimacy. The intimacy is what brings the freedom. When we know Him as He knows us, the veil is removed from our eyes and we see Him and know Him. That first look is like no other but the intimacy grows in relationship. Face to face we grow more like Him as we spend facetime with Him. Unlike Facebook or FaceTime, this face to face isn't a video call or chat. This face to face time is an intimate introduction and interaction of the King of Glory with His bride. My husband and I as well as both of our boys had long distance relationships prior to marriage. These are hard but boy was it more difficult before cell phones. My youngest bemoans the time he is away from his girlfriend and I try to explain that he has it so much better than we did because he can see her face and hear her voice through FaceTime but the truth is that intimacy comes through the knowing. FaceTime isn't enough. Investing time to spend face to face, in personal relationship matters. The same is to be said with this lover of our soul. We cannot count on intimacy with God unless we invest face to face time in The Word and with Him in intimate relationship. This God who was, is the God who Is and always will be. Time is now to make some face to face time with Him.

Moses spoke to the people: "Don't be afraid. Stand firm and watch God do his work of salvation for you today. Take a good look at the Egyptians today for you're never going to see them again. God will fight the battle for you. And you? You keep your mouths shut!" - Exodus 14: 13-14

Are you so caught up in your circumstances that you stopped looking forward to your miracle in the making?

Have you forgotten what He's already done for you?

Key thought for today:

Peace & Quiet!

Often we get our noses out of joint with God and feel like He is leaving us to fight our own battles or isn't doing as He promised when the reality is that we are looking in the wrong direction. As a different preacher presented at our church, he challenged my thought processes on the way we look at God's provision. He talked about the miracles of the Red Sea crossing and how it was more than one miracle and as I envisioned it in my mind, I realized that I am too often like these Israelites murmuring against God as I look back at the clouds of destruction headed my way instead of looking forward to the miracle in the making. I often wish I was at the front of the line of miracles instead of the end. I mean, those at the front saw the miracle first as they stepped into the sea bed onto dry land. On the other side, they were further away when the sea closed over the Egyptians so they missed a spectacular demonstration of God's awesomeness there too. I think we too often are so caught up in our circumstances or so busy dodging the things that are throwing curveballs at us that we miss the miracle in the making. We are an incredibly blessed people but we get so bogged down in our wants that we forget our haves. We get so frustrated with our desires not being met that we forget all our blessings we have seen and the places He has brought us out from. Here we sit, our problems, coming after us like those pursuing the people at that time and we are looking at the dust-clouds heading our way rather than turning our back on that to look at Him and the miracle of the sea parting before us. Moses spoke to the people and said, take a good look at the problems for you are never going to see them again. God is going to fight this battle for you. Meanwhile, you? Stop your complaining and keep your mouth shut to your whining. God is in control. Whatever is happening to you right now, turn it over to God. Turn your back on it and begin to look towards Him as He parts the sea instead of focusing on the problems chasing after you. Look ahead to all that He has and begin to sing of His wonders instead of whining about your current circumstances. Praise will be my song.

Good people last—they can't be moved; the wicked are here today, gone tomorrow.
A good person's mouth is a clear fountain of wisdom; a foul mouth is a stagnant swamp.
The speech of a good person clears the air the words of the wicked pollute it.
Proverbs 10: 30-32

We are called to be a support to others. When you give to others despite your pain, how does this affect you?

Is there someone you can reach out to today?

Key thought for today:

Down, Not Out!

The picture of this tree speaks a million words to me on so many levels because it lives despite being undercut as it is grafted and held by the outstretched arms of the neighboring tree. This is a picture of what being rooted in God is and how we are called to be this support for those around us. When I first looked at this picture, my mind was focused on how the larger tree took on the smaller one, supporting it after it was obviously undercut but then I looked again. The smaller tree has evidence of growth all over it where it branched out, constantly networking, connecting, growing and supporting the other trees around it. You see growth isn't just how big you are but it is in your connections, the leaves and branches that collect the sun and the dew and the nutrients from the air. The larger tree has benefited from the smaller tree because it has grown and become more from its support of the smaller tree. In Proverbs, the wise king Solomon says good people last and their words are a clear fountain of wisdom that clears the air. Trees give life as they absorb the carbon dioxide we put off and they create oxygen for us to breathe. God created an interdependent network of life for us here on Earth in His wisdom and knowledge. He knows we need each other and that need is vital to our existence. The need causes us to branch out to others for support and to help. That need can cause grief. You can be undercut and hurt but you can also be supported and supportive. The more you branch out, the more you connect, the more you'll see and experience pain and heartache but you will also grow in confidence and strength, life and purpose. Hurt comes but so do the vital nutrients of life. Good people last. They connect and keep reaching no matter the pain. They branch out giving life to others and getting life in return because they are interwoven into the fabric of life itself. God gives us clear and visible evidence all around us of the incredible necessity of being interwoven from the fungus of the ground that is essential to our being to the very air produced by the trees He created before He created man. We are purposed. We are important and necessary. You may feel hurt, undercut, cut off and unnecessary but I am telling you now that you are vital. You are exactly what God created for this time and this place. Never doubt that He has purposed you. Hurting means you are alive. Reach out. Connect. Support someone else. Network. Your life giving support to another despite your pain will in turn give you life. Find another to love on from your place of pain and watch the network of life breathe life back into you. You may feel cut down but I promise, you are not out. You are a necessary part of life and you are able to be a difference. Being the difference for someone else will in turn make a difference in your own life. Don't stop giving. Don't give up because you have been hurt. Keep breathing life because it matters and your words clear the pollution that others have put out. Your support means the difference to someone even if it feels like it doesn't. Be the fountain of wisdom, the supporter of others and the good that keeps networking despite the hurt. Through the pain comes life and you will last while those who are only out for themselves will fade away.

But the Master said, "You don't need more faith. There is no 'more' or 'less' in faith. If you have a bare kernel of faith, say the size of a poppy seed, you could say to this sycamore tree, 'Go jump in the lake,' and it would do it. - Luke 17: 6

Here's a question to ask yourself: is your desire for having more or being more in line with your willingness to do more, sacrifice more, give more, etc. Are you willing to stand out and be the MORE or are you just wanting the more?

Faith isn't about more as He says a tiny seed is enough. The question is what are we doing with the amount we have?

Key thought for today:

More!

"So the Lord said, "If you have faith as a mustard seed, you can say to this mulberry tree, 'Be pulled up by the roots and be planted in the sea,' and it would obey you."

Luke 17:6 NKJV

Ok. I get it. The difference of interpretation affected your thoughts...you got stuck on the poppy seed over the mustard seed or the sycamore tree over the mulberry bush, and....you missed the point. The point isn't about the size of faith or even the problem in front of you, it is the trust and action. See we always tend to want more. This is why advertising and the world appeal to that in us. What we have is never enough. God had given the whole Garden to Adam and Eve but they still allowed the desire for "more" to steal what they had. More desire isn't always a bad thing but it can certainly be a distracting thing. Here's a question to ask yourself: is your desire for having more or being more in line with your willingness to do more, sacrifice more, give more, etc. Are you willing to stand out and be the MORE or are you just wanting the more? Jesus said we don't need more as there is no more or less of faith or Him. I love the song More of You because it expresses my desire to be closer but More of God is only possible if there is less of Me consuming or filling up my desires. More is a human desire or trait. More is a false sense. More isn't about Him, more is about us and that is the problem. Faith isn't about more as He says a tiny seed is enough. The question is what are we doing with the amount we have? Are we planting? Watering? Fertilizing? Are we reaching out, sowing and harvesting? Are we being the more that we wish we had? If there is a problem in your way, what are you doing about it? Are you speaking truth over it? Are you actively doing something about it or are you just whining and wanting? Whether it is a poppy seed or a mustard seed doesn't matter. Whether it is a sycamore tree or a mulberry bush or a mountain or whatever type of problem doesn't matter. What matters is the action. What are you doing with what you have?

Jesus said, "Were not ten healed? Where are the nine? Can none be found to come back and give glory to God except this outsider?" Then he said to him, "Get up. On your way. Your faith has healed and saved you." - Luke 17: 17-19

Are you living, walking daily in complete awareness of His presence or have you strayed away, carrying your scars with you?

Why do we miss out on His Completeness?

Key thought for today:

The Art of Remembrance!

What a fine compliment it is when someone remembers you in time of need or pain, celebrating Or congratulations but even more just in remembering. A sweet simple flower picked from a garden, a warm thank you card mailed at the right time, or a sentimental gift made by hand says "I care" loudly. Loving loud is as simple as taking the time to listen to another, pray for them and/or just being there. There are many times in life that we cannot be enough for others or we feel stretched thin. The worldly societal demands pull and tug until we are misshapen and out of sorts in our minds and hearts so often that we feel stressed and like giving up but we must remember the art. You see a rose is not a rose until it is first a bud. The art of remembrance takes time to develop and it requires purpose. We often fail in keeping up with all because we don't prioritize and try to keep juggling instead. This is a season of remembrance and thankfulness. This is a time where we need to slow down and take the time to be deliberate about saying thank you. Thank you God for sending your son. Thank you for the sunrise and the beautiful day. Thank you for remembering me when I have forgotten myself. The flowers bloom fragrantly and their beauty is incomparable. The intricacies of the unfolding bud and fragrance isn't my doing. My job is just to enjoy the fragrance and the sight but also to remember the thorns. See, if I get so caught up in the beauty and fragrance that I carelessly reach out, I will catch a thorn in my hand or bruise the rose. This is often what happens when we try to grab onto that moment or thing that's so attractive to us. We end up hurt or hurting others instead of taking the time to appreciate and steep in the art of remembrance. Jesus healed ten lepers. Leprosy is a bad viral infection called Legionnaires' disease. What we often miss in this passage is the completeness. You see when lepers had this bad sickness, they had to go into quarantining areas to protect others from catching it. Once they got over it, if they did, then they had to go present themselves to the priest so he could declare them clean and allow them back in. The bad thing is that they got scars and often lost body parts while the disease raged. Jesus healed the ten lepers who were begging for healing. He took away the disease and off they went to get their declaration of clean from the priest but only one truly got it right. One had the art of remembrance and it paid off in completeness. I don't know the stage of his/her disease and I don't know much detail about this one nor the others but I do know that Jesus stated that the faith of the one healed and saved him. No matter which version we read, two things stand out. The healing was made complete by the art of remembering to say thank you and it was the act of a person not from the area. I can only imagine them visiting the area, becoming sick and then stuck. I can only imagine how that disease had struck their life making it impossible to move forward. In a foreign land, now an outcast and losing all hope, then Jesus arrives. Wow! How many times have I been stuck in an awkward, impossible situation with no hope and The Master reached out to touch me! The thing is that the scars and healing, the completeness of salvation and total deliverance are there if we will but learn the art of gratitude in remembrance. Thankfulness. Faith filled appreciation for the touch from the Master restored this leper to life and more, eternal life. He/She was saved and made completely whole. I cannot help but feel sorry for those who in their rush to get the healing verified, missed out on the completeness of restoration and a scar free life. They took their remembrance with them and missed out on their wholeness. They took their scars and their burdens of memory with them. They were healed from this disease but missed the completeness all because they failed to recognize the High Priest was in their presence. Lord, let me become so aware of your presence that I continually walk in your completeness. I don't want to carry my scars of old hurts around. I want to walk in complete forgiveness and wholeness. Thank you Jesus for the blood you shed. Thank you Jesus that you have declared that by your stripes we are healed. Remind my heart of your completeness and help me to walk in the art of remembrance so I may be whole, unscarred by the stains and thorns of life. Let me experience your beauty and fragrance of your presence without bruising your heart by my careless ways. I want to be the one who walks in fullness of healing and hope, not a shadow of myself, carrying scars of the past but whole and complete in you! Thank you Lord for all!

When God, your God, ushers you into the land he promised through your ancestors Abraham, Isaac, and Jacob to give you, you're going to walk into large, bustling cities you didn't build, well-furnished houses you didn't buy, come upon wells you didn't dig, vineyards and olive orchards you didn't plant. When you take it all in and settle down, pleased and content, make sure you don't forget how you got there—God brought you out of slavery in Egypt. - Deuteronomy 6:10-12

Are you living, walking daily in complete awareness of His presence or have you strayed away, carrying your scars with you?

Why do we miss out on His Completeness?

Key thought for today:

Don't Forget!

First, we need to have a lesson in grammar. Remember is to pull into consciousness while don't forget means to hold in awareness. In the original Greek/Hebrew as within many other languages, these are completely different actions. Forget means to put away or never think of again as in when God forgives our sins, He actually puts them away to never be remembered-forgotten-as far as the East is from the West-infinitely gone. To "not forget" is the opposite which means to hold in constant awareness so it doesn't slip away from our minds. There are several times when God instructed people to "not forget". Once is our context for today and another is to not forget the bride of your youth. Why are these so important? Why not just say remember as used in other connotations? The details matter. The Bible uses "remember" over 1200 times but "don't forget" is used only around 300. This is a whole sermon series for someone! To remember is to call from memory and God tells us to put things in our memory like His word-hidden in our heart- so we can remember them. He tells Moses to build an altar of rocks to remember after the crossing of the Red Sea. Remember is to call back and focus on but Don't forget... well that means more. Unfortunately, though God instructed the people in Deuteronomy to Don't forget how they got to the place of fulfillment in their lives....they did! We do too! We are instructed to not forget because God knows if we do not hold it in constant awareness we are prone to forgetfulness-we deprioritize it and then it shifts from our focus. When is the last time you "didn't forget" something? You know what I mean. You are headed to the store and you must remember what you need so you made a conscious effort to "not forget" rather than just to remember because if you didn't, you might forget. That was fun wasn't it! Not forgetting for we humans is a job of constant awareness and extra effort in order to hold that thought. When God instructs us to Don't forget, He wants us to hold it in our minds constantly.

Do Not Forget God. Hold Him constantly in your presence-not on the back shelf where He is pulled out and remembered sometimes but constantly dwelling in your mind/heart!
""Beware that you do not forget the Lord your God by not keeping His commandments, His judgments, and His statutes which I command you today," Deuteronomy 8:11 NKJV
"But do not forget to do good and to share, for with such sacrifices God is well pleased."

Hebrews 13:16 NKJV

But me, I'm not giving up. I'm sticking around to see what God will do.
I'm waiting for God to make things right.
I'm counting on God to listen to me. - Micah 7:7

Are you struggling in a situation today and feel as if you've been forgotten?

How can we trust that God is always there, no matter what?

Key thought for today:

Confident Peace!

Right now as I sit here, I am struggling to breathe fully from the car accident I was in yesterday. My back and side were impacted greatly and my knees are black and blue like my upper torso but I am so blessed. I'm not giving up! God kept me from death, permanent disability and so much more. God will do amazing things even though the struggle feels real in the moment. As I felt the bump from behind that launched me into the intersection, all I thought was Jesus...and said oh no. My husband was on the hands free phone and heard the entire incident so I can only imagine his fright. As my car careened around the intersection being hit repeatedly by other cars like a bumper car, I could only think, Jesus. And it truly is a miracle. My car is totaled but my body is not. I was taken by ambulance in incredible pain but another miracle occurred then. I saw my neighbor's son, a friend, who was there helping me. I heard his voice in the midst of my anxiety. God had sent him to me in that moment. He doesn't usually work that area and was on overtime. God sent him. All through the surreal experience, God had moments of His glory, from the opportunity to pray over the first responders to the opportunity to pray with the woman who had the blood issue in my ER room. My nurse was married to the PA of my back doctor and I got to share with him. All through the day, each and every touchpoint, God was real. I am waiting on God to make it right, counting on Him to hear me and listen. He knows me and has me in His hand. In Micah, the prophet reminds us of this. I am not giving up. I am sticking around to see what God will do-not can do or may do but Will do. Counting on God! Confident that He knows my situation before I do. I may be sore and beaten up. My car will not ever be the same again but God knows me and my situation before I do. He is ready and able. I am in confident peace with His ways. Walking in confident peace with Him. Feeling a confident peace as I know Him! He knows my name and He knows yours too! My airbag didn't deploy but my seatbelt left a definite impression on my body. It held me in that moment just as it was intended to do. God held me too. In that moment and every moment since, God has held me. I don't know your trial but I do know He holds you too! That's just who He is. Peace isn't the absence of problems but rather the complete confidence in those moments that no matter what your situation, He knows your name!

Look! Striding across the mountains— a messenger bringing the latest good news:
peace! A holiday, Judah! Celebrate! Worship and recommit to God!
No more worries about this enemy. This one is history. Close the books. - Nahum 1:15

Why is it that when we are held captive to pain or discomfort or discouragement or stress, we tend to look at the situation rather than rest in the Who He is?

How can we come to a place of celebrating peace?

Key thought for today:

Celebrate Peace!

Ears ringing, noise clanging, stressed body and lots of pain signals many things wrong, but the truth is that life is full of all things wrong. Yet we can celebrate peace despite the wrong. It is easy to count the bad, in fact, it seems to be what makes the most clamor, from moment to moment. In Nahum, we are instructed to Look! Look for peace. Look for good news. Celebrate, worship and recommit to God! No more worries about this enemy you are fighting! Whether that enemy be cancer or financial issues, health, wealth or emotional struggles, God has declared for you to celebrate His peace. Take a holiday from your worry and just be confident in Him. Look for His answers striding across the mountains. Too often we get into a hurry and miss out on what God has for us. Life isn't always fair, in fact, I used to tell my students that life isn't fair at all. Fair isn't equal. Fair isn't having what everyone else has or doesn't have. It is so easy to get distracted and discouraged by all the bad. In this chapter of Nahum, the author was first looking at all the problems with Nineveh. He was counting all the issues and talking about God being serious business then his tone changed to the graciousness of God. Nineveh is located in modern day Iraq. The history of war and trouble from the Assyrians of that region towards Israel is noted. Nineveh was a city of wealth and pride, prosperity and indulgence but also a place of violence and great sin. Nineveh was the capital of this region and a draw/attraction to many youth. The peace couldn't be had as long as the enemy was perceived to be winning. But here Nahum is declaring that the enemy is unimportant. The battle is over. Close the books and quit allowing the vocalists of that power to take hold, instead look to God who is striding across the mountains declaring the victory. When you are held captive to pain or discomfort or discouragement or stress, you tend to look at the situation rather than rest in the Who He is. It is easier to look at circumstances than to know. But it is in the knowing that peace is had. Celebrate before the end is declared. Worship and recommit to God with complete confidence that He is working all things out. Don't let the trials of life steal your joy. Look! Take a holiday from your worry and relax in who He is. He is the Peace who has broken down every wall.

> *Since this is the kind of life we have chosen, the life of the Spirit, let us make sure that we do not just hold it as an idea in our heads or a sentiment in our hearts, but work out its implications in every detail of our lives. That means we will not compare ourselves with each other as if one of us were better and another worse. We have far more interesting things to do with our lives. Each of us is an original.*
> **Galatians 5:25**

We have chosen the life but are we living it out or are we just second guessing ourselves at every turn?

How do we dwell in His peace, tranquility, contentment and rest?

Key thought for today:

An Original!

Some Days it is easy to get discouraged by the flow of life and its ups and downs. This devotional has been percolating all day long as I dwelt on His goodness and fought with my weaknesses from injury all day. The choice. This verse says, since this is the kind of life we have chosen, the life of the Spirit, let us make sure....well, you can read but here it is...the choice. We have chosen the life but are we living it out or are we just second guessing ourselves at every turn? See, ideas in our heads often get left behind or neglected just like sentiments in our hearts. We feel them and they fade. We don't act on them. When we constantly compare ourselves with one another, we often waste time that is better spent doing more interesting things. As I think about life, I embrace the statement Paul made to the Galatians, we are all originals. An original is unique, one of a kind, created with purpose and special. God calls us each originals and says not to compare our lives to others, yet that is exactly what we do. This constant comparison keeps us from true contentment because we can never measure up to our perception of what others have. We always see the grass as greener or their lives as easier or better. The more we stew on what another has or does, the more discontent breeds into our lives. Holding onto the idea of a life of peace and contentment without acting on it means we are constantly waiting on something that is already ours. Peace, tranquility, contentment and rest are already ours in God's complete love. There is no greater gift, no greater possession, and no greater satisfaction than to dwell in this love. How do we make this our home? We work out its implications in every detail of our lives. It is a work constantly in progress. The picture this scripture is posted on is the birth and death of a star. It is the beginning and the ending all in one photo. When an idea is first conceived, it is a thought and nothing more but as the details are fleshed out and worked on and made into essence, it becomes. The Spirit life is not just an idea nor just a feeling in our heart but a work in progress that we must walk out each and every moment. Everything in our lives becomes a beacon or a piece of the puzzle to this masterpiece. The broken parts and the messes, the celebrations and the rewards all become an intricate detail with implications upon our lives. One of my favorite songs of all time is I am a promise. It states that I am a great big bundle of potentiality! As we learn and lean, it becomes evident that He has purposed us with great potential but we must learn to walk and work out the intricacies by following in His love. Quit living a life of comparison and start living a life of love. Work out the intricacies of His love step by step, day by day and trust Him to be the one who makes the star! Choose the life, not the idea of the life. Life, not the sentiment. The life that is far more interesting as an original! Not limitations, only possibilities!

Your beauty and love chase after me every day of my life.
I'm back home in the house of God for the rest of my life.
Psalms 23:6

Why is it that when we are held captive to pain or discomfort or discouragement or stress, we tend to look at the situation rather than rest in the Who He is?

How can we come to a place of celebrating peace?

Key thought for today:

Beautiful Peace!

I love the 23rd Psalms for many reasons but verse 6 in The Message version is a top one. When life has kicked me, beaten me down and tried to steal my joy, this verse reminds me of the truth. His beauty and love chase after me daily and I can be at rest in His house any time I want. I do not have to allow the cares of life to be my comeuppance nor do I have to measure up to anyone's standards or expectations. My only purpose is in Him. I do not have to be judged nor judge anyone else. I do not have to run after others because He is running after me. His truth is my character. His beauty is in my mirror. His love is my dwelling place. His home is my home. No matter what my body is saying in its aches and groans nor what others say, my beautiful peace is at home in Him. I can just turn it all over to Him and He will. This verse is a balm in a hurting place for someone. Read it again then rest in it. His beautiful peace is chasing after you to wrap you in His loving arms. Quit running and let Him catch you in His loving arms. Be at home in Him no matter what your circumstances say. He is love, He is joy, He is peace.

Be cheerful no matter what; pray all the time; thank God no matter what happens. This is the way God wants you who belong to Christ Jesus to live. - 1 Thessalonians 5:16-18

Is it possible to live every day in joy, peace and love?

What is the key to a life of fulfillment?

Key thought for today:

Cheerful Peace!

Is it possible to live every day in joy, peace and love? Jesus said it was and is. He said that no matter what happens we can have cheer or joy by walking in a thankful life. I have seen the stark contrast of walking in gratitude versus walking in the life of poor me. One, being down all the time is exhausting mentally and physically as well as a chore to be around. Cheerful peace is a choice. Paul writes to the church to be cheerful no matter what; pray all the time; thank God no matter what happens. Why? Because this is the way of blessing and happiness. It is the key to unlocking a life of fulfillment. When you walk in gratitude, your life exudes Him no matter what. You are joy filled. You are a magnet to others and you draw goodness to yourself because you walk in His glory. Note that I don't say life is perfect without issues. It is a mindset of choice. No matter what comes my way, I choose joy. I choose to be of good cheer not because my problems don't exist but because I know He is working all things out for my good. I am not lost without hope because greater is He that is in me. Life may dish out tough things and it often does, but it is my choice to give it to Him in gratitude and praise or hold onto it until it makes me bitter and stinky. I can celebrate the goodness which reflects who He is or I can sit around whining about my wishes that weren't met or my problems until I am a hot stinky mess of bitterness. I would rather a hundred days of pain living in gratitude for what He has done than one day of wealth in a pile of stinginess. God wants to bless and be good to all who belong to Him. He uses our trials to develop us in character and love. I know I have had my fair share of trials but I can choose joy through them and it is much more pleasant to walk through a trial in gratitude than in a miserable attitude. Praying all the time for His will and direction is the true path to success and wisdom. Wealth and beauty as defined by this world fades quickly but a person who walks in gratitude will last forever as they dwell in the place of the Most High. He who creates the stars knows us by name. When you wake up in pain, it is a choice to walk in praise or pity. When a catastrophe happens, you have a choice of seeing the good or the bad. Be cheerful. This means to choose gratitude, cheer, joy and a life in Him no matter what. It is a choice but it is His command so I choose cheerful peace in knowing that greater is He that is in me than He that is in this world. I choose His cheer when my world has been rocked by sorrow. I choose His cheerful peace no matter what!

Oh, thank God—he's so good! His love never runs out.
All of you set free by God, tell the world! Tell how he freed you from
oppression, Then rounded you up from all over the place,
from the four winds, from the seven seas. - Psalms 107:1-3

We are not immune from problems in this life, so how can we be a reflection of His peace, His promises through our trials?

In what ways can we express our gratitude for His goodness and mercy?

Key thought for today:

Rainbow of Peace!

I love the rainbow because it is a fascinating and real example of God's promise that comes after the rain and only because of the water in the atmosphere. In Psalms, David has reached the pinnacle of His life and yet he still has issues and problems. He tells us to thank God. He is so good! His love never runs out. I always read this before as an address to a group of people but as I read it today as a message to me, it suddenly jumped out. I have been so scattered feeling, so overwhelmed and mentally fractured into a million thoughts that when I read "He rounds you up", it spoke volumes to me. As we celebrate this season of thanksgiving, it is important to recognize that this fractious self can be pulled together into a rainbow of beauty as we allow His light to shine through our storms. It may feel like you are constantly in the rain but remember that He is always there as the Son to shine through you and the water vapor of tears from the struggles is the making of the rainbow of promise as you lean into Him. No one goes through life without problems. Wealth doesn't make you immune, health doesn't make you immune, even wisdom and God's perfect love doesn't make you immune from troubles. In this world, we all have troubles. But scripture says, be of good cheer-find the Son to reflect-because He has overcome the world, the storm, the pain, and the sorrow. He has overcome death, hell and the grave. He has conquered all. Our role is to rest in Him and allow His rainbow of peace that passes all understanding to refract the light of His love despite the storm-because of the storm-through the rain to become the promise. His love endures forever, never runs out and is freedom! Dwell there in your deepest storm so others can know His love reflected in you through your storms. Be the rainbow of promise and peace by leaning into His love through the storm.

Let the peace of Christ keep you in tune with each other, in step with each other. None of this going off and doing your own thing. And cultivate thankfulness. Let the Word of Christ—the Message—have the run of the house. Give it plenty of room in your lives. Instruct and direct one another using good common sense. And sing, sing your hearts out to God! Let every detail in your lives—words, actions, whatever—be done in the name of the Master, Jesus, thanking God the Father every step of the way. - Colossians 3:15-17

It is so easy to lose your song, your harmony and your tune when you are not giving the things of God plenty of room in your life. How are we to stay in sync with God?

How does the peace of Christ differ from the world's peace?

Key thought for today:

Peaceful Tune!

Out of sync, out of touch, out of tune, and disharmonious are the ways some days, weeks, months and even some years can be described. Like wading through a marsh of quicksand, carefully and painfully, life can tear at one bringing the cares of life down like a weight stealing one's breath. It is so easy when you are struggling, to lash out at one another tearing and pulling, tugging and fighting. In Colossians, Paul writes that we are to let the peace of Christ keep us in tune with one another. It is easy to take off on our own way, doing our own thing. This is human nature and the path that leads to sin and disharmony. It leads to an attitude of ungratefulness and sucks at the very essence of who God has called us to be. In the beginning of time, the woman Eve was not in companionship with Adam at the time of the temptation. She had gone off alone and was deceived because she wasn't in sync with her spouse. I am not saying you can never do things alone but I am saying that disharmony breeds disconnection and discontent. If you are not allowing instruction and direction from one another using good common sense and Godly thankfulness, you are not in sync, in step, in communion with the things of God. It is so easy to lose your song, your harmony and your tune when you are not giving the things of God plenty of room in your lives. When you put the things of God into a small box that is only brought out to go to church, bitterness and frustration with the church itself will creep in. The whole song of peace will become a song of anger and be like clanging symbols. Living a life of disruption leads to a life of disappointment and despair. Paul says we are instead to sing through our problems allowing every detail in our lives-our words, our actions, our deeds, our dreams, our desires, whatever-be done in the name of Jesus. How different our world would be if we applied this one thing. When our lives become too busy for thankfulness, too busy for gratitude, too busy for our song to be sung to Him, then we fall out of sync and out of love with Him. We become jaded and hard to be around. We lose out on His blessings because we get out of step with Him. We become caught up in our own paths, desires and happiness losing sight of who He is. Perfect pitch doesn't happen by accident. Harmony isn't uninstructed. Life has a natural tune with ebb and flow. God set this pattern in place. When this cycle becomes disrupted by the chaos of our own ways and our own minds instead of in sync with Him, the melody of life is played in selfishness instead of love. If we want a peaceful tune in our lives, we must stay in step with each other not by trying to keep up and compare ourselves to others but to cultivate thankfulness and our songs. Let praise and gratitude be your song, instead of harsh words and criticism. Let sweet words and melodies play a soft answer to the harsh words of another, then God's answer will reign. I don't understand why bad things happen. I do agree that life is often unfair but we can choose to be thankful and grateful in praise for who He is or we can go our own way in disharmony, missing out on the peaceful tune of life. Every song I have heard that rings true, has places of notes that are sharp or flat. These hard places in the tune make the harmonies so much more beautiful. Life brings pain and sorrows and suffering because we live in an imperfect world. We get the choice to stay with the song and continue in praise and thanksgiving despite the struggle to reach the peaceful crescendo. We can choose to let the peace of Christ keep us in tune and in step with one another. We can choose to let the details of our lives be lived in the name and honor of Christ as a peaceful tune. We can choose to give it place in our homes and our lives by cultivating thankfulness. It is our choice. We can choose our songs. Praise will be my song.

God bless you and keep you, God smile on you and gift you,
God look you full in the face and make you prosper. - Numbers 6:24-26

What is the definition of prosperous peace?

What is the difference in prosperity and wealth?

Key thought for today:

Prosperous Peace!

Misunderstood. Words said, written, texted, etc are often misunderstood but these words are God's words given from God to Moses with instructions that these are the words the priests should use to bless His people. There is no greater blessing than to know that God smiles on you, blesses you, keeps you, gifts you and looks you full in the face to make you prosper. This is the definition of prosperous peace. Knowing that God looks at you fully in the face with His blessings upon you. These are not words that can be mistakenly said nor can this promise be taken away. God isn't a confused God nor can these words be misunderstood or misinterpreted. Science can be doctored or misinterpreted but God cannot. His word is infallible. It doesn't change with your circumstances nor does it only apply to some and not to others. His word is His promise. His promise is ours as His children. He doesn't depart from His word. Time changes, people change, situations change, circumstances change, but God never changes. The moon is the moon despite the seasons and the portion we can see or the amount of light it reflects. God said, "Let there be light" and until He declares differently the sun and the moon will function in His authority. Once we grasp this fully that He has looked us full in the face and our prosperity is His, then we can quit worrying about how we are going to make it and rest in His prosperous peace. Prosperity isn't about wealth. Prosperity is successful well being, a sense of thriving and success. If we find our well being in Him and His ways, then all the other will follow. Wealth doesn't bring happiness and poverty doesn't cause sadness. This mindset is what causes men's hearts to tremble and fall into sin in order to preserve their lifestyle. Imagine saying this promise over your children every day. It is the job of the priest to speak it over the children of Israel, and we live in the new covenant where Jesus is the fulfillment of all the old and the promise of all the new. Begin to speak His promises, His life, His prosperous peace over your children as we walk in His authority as priests over our households. Speak the name of Jesus over those hurting, in sorrow and in pain. Speak Him and His promises, then watch His promises being fulfilled because they are His.

God is love. When we take up permanent residence in a life of love, we live in God and God lives in us. This way, love has the run of the house, becomes at home and mature in us, so that we're free of worry on Judgment Day—our standing in the world is identical with Christ's. There is no room in love for fear. Well-formed love banishes fear. Since fear is crippling, a fearful life—fear of death, fear of judgment—is one not yet fully formed in love. - 1 John 4:17-18

If you are struggling with complete peace, how/where can you begin to find it?

What steps can we take to grow in love and thus experience freedom from fear?

Key thought for today:

Complete Peace!

Fear torments and steals peace. Fear is crippling and limiting. Fear of life, fear of death, fear of judgment, fear of failure, fear of success, fear of suffering, fear of pain, fear torments and fear, like darkness, permeates. But love like light banishes fear. God is love and when we take up residence in Him, we live a life of Love. Love runs through us and becomes at home in a tangible way that others see. We become worry free and mature in God when we begin to walk in His love fully. Trust and complete peace only come with total confidence in God. You cannot have total confidence unless there is first, knowing. If you do not know someone, you cannot trust. If you are not confident or sure of a person, you are not fully walking in a full relationship or complete peace with that person. When your relationship is unstable or unsure, when there are emotional upheavals and distrust, there is a lack of peace. Recently I saw a friend, who has been fighting cancer vigorously, post that she was making memories. She is fighting to make a legacy of memories for her family because she has been told that her lifetime is short. She has been given a time frame and she has decided to live life fully during that time. The truth is that we have all been given a time frame. Some of us know that time is short and others do not know that date but today could be that day. Peace wins when we give up our fear of the future and decide to embrace it no matter how long it is. Peace isn't the absence of worry or the absence of problems. Peace is confidence through the situations. Peace is making memories knowing that this moment might be the last or the first of many. Peace is a surety that no matter what happens, the best moment will win out. The confidence that this life isn't all there is nor is it the only life. One moment can change your life forever. It can be a moment of victory or defeat and only you can decide that. The moment that changes our lives is the moment we decide to walk in love and light rather than fear and darkness. The moment that makes our lives more is when we give up the control of making ourselves happy to making memories in love. Life is but a series of moments. Life can be full of problems or full of memories. The problems of yesterday can be the promise of tomorrow filled with memories. As we stood around talking with family a few days ago, I realized that things that were hairy scary moments are now funny memories. Things that were once things that took my breath away are just reflections of moments lived. Our lives are fleeting whether we know our death date or not. A car accident, an unexpected circumstance, a disease or a sudden sickness can take things to a whole different level of life but our complete Peace doesn't come because we are not struggling with these things. Our complete peace comes in the knowledge that no matter what comes our way, He has overcome. He already knows our future. He already knows. As my life flashed in front of my eyes while the car spun out of my control, I suddenly understood. I cannot control my future. I cannot control the ups and downs, but I can control my reaction to them. I can control myself. I can walk in love no matter what. God is love. We must take up permanent residence in a life of love. Mature love is complete peace. When God's love is walking fully in you, then you will know complete peace.

Friends, when life gets really difficult, don't jump to the conclusion that God isn't on the job. Instead, be glad that you are in the very thick of what Christ experienced. This is a spiritual refining process, with glory just around the corner - 1 Peter 4:12-13.

What is refined peace? How do we achieve it?

Are you in the refining process of peace? What are you doing to help get through the process?

Key thought for today:

Refined Peace!

The process of anything done is the place of learning. The outcome is often what we focus on when the focus should be on the process. I watched a documentary the other day on the refining process of sugar-had no idea it was so dangerous! In fact, refining sugar causes a lot of fires. Sugar dust is combustible and when it swirls in the air while being refined, it can catch fire so extreme caution must be used. Sugar is a potential form of energy to our bodies but also addictive and also can be terribly bad for us as it easily converts to fat. Sugar or Sucralose is also necessary to our bodies so we crave it, want it, desire it a lot. When life gets difficult, we want more of what we do not need. We crave an end or a solution; desire a resolution and peace. When life is difficult, it is easy to assume that God has let us down or isn't doing as He promised because we are human and see things simplistically and desire immediacy. The refining process of the spiritual life is just as combustible as refining sugar. When we are being refined, it is easy to jump to conclusions and explode as the dust particles of the process overwhelm our lives. It is easy to get confused by the dust of the work in progress and fail to see the outcome. Refined peace comes through the process not the outcome. Peace is a confidence in the process, the knowledge that the outcome will be perfect in God's timing despite the dust clouds of the refining process. It is easy in the process to jump to the conclusion that God has forgotten us. David did it, Moses did it, in fact, I cannot think of anyone that didn't do it. We like to think that we are the only ones who get down, discouraged or disappointed with God's timing and purposes but it is a part of the process. It is the refining part, the most combustible part. It is the part that works peace and patience in us developing the fruit of the Spirit. If your life seems to be like a ticking time bomb waiting to explode, then it is time to rejoice for you are in the refining process of peace. God is working in you and on you so that refined peace-the kind that passes all understanding-will define your life. This is the time to rejoice that you are in the very thick of what Christ Himself experienced. This is the spiritual refining process that results in the sweetness of glory. When the dust clears and settles, the glory remains to be seen. Don't jump to the conclusion that God isn't working, instead begin to realize that the God of the impossible is doing what only He can do! Just begin to celebrate as the clouds clear! Rejoice that the process is underway in the refining. The refined peace will be worth it. The glory. The more than you think or ask...is in the waiting. Embrace the process of the refining because it leads to His glory!

Remember: A stingy planter gets a stingy crop; a lavish planter gets a lavish crop. I want each of you to take plenty of time to think it over, and make up your own mind what you will give. That will protect you against sob stories and arm-twisting. God loves it when the giver delights in the giving. - 2 Corinthians 9:6-7

How are we to give?

What is the blessing for giving cheerfully?

Key thought for today:

Peaceful Giving!

Take plenty of time. Think it over. Make up your own mind about what you will give. These are the instructions from Paul to the church. This time of year, there is so much pressure on the buying and giving that people miss the point or message. They miss the knowing that God is a God of blessings and not just a little but a lot. He is so faithful to us despite ourselves. The psalmist continues by saying: "God can pour on the blessings in astonishing ways so that you're ready for anything and everything, more than just ready to do what needs to be done. As one psalmist puts it, He throws caution to the winds, giving to the needy in reckless abandon. His right-living, right-giving ways never run out, never wear out.

2 Corinthians 9:8-9 MSG

God doesn't want us to give out of obligation or debt but rather with delight and excitement that we have the opportunity to give. He doesn't bless us to bless Himself. He blesses those who sow as they sow. If you are stingy in your giving and your ways are to give but do it with a mouthy spirit or with strings attached, He sees this. God wants us to be delighted while being able to help others, to give and to be a blessing. When we approach our life as a blessing, and an offering to him, He lavishly pours out His blessings upon us. Sometimes it is hard for us to see the blessings because we get so busy looking at the problems and we forget to count all the wonderful things that he's done. Generosity equals lavish blessings but we don't do it because we get but rather because we love because love delights in giving!

So, my very dear friends, don't get thrown off course. Every desirable and beneficial gift comes out of heaven. The gifts are rivers of light cascading down from the Father of Light. There is nothing deceitful in God, nothing two-faced, nothing fickle. He brought us to life using the true Word, showing us off as the crown of all his creatures. - James 1: 16-18

Out of everything God created, we are considered to be what?

What is the purpose, course and reason for our lives?

Key thought for today:

Crowned!

Life often throws us curve balls hoping to get us off course but the concept of staying in the Light is possible if we remember who He is. God brought us to life using the true Word. Our life was not light until He came as the river of light cascading down from the Father of Light to show us the way of the desirable and beneficial gifts of life. When someone gets a gift for another, there is no assurance that that particular gift is the perfect, desired and beneficial gift. This is not the case with God. He knows exactly what we need and the when/how even when we do not. He knows us so well that He has designed and put into place the right gifts at the right times for our lives. We are the crown of all His creation. When we look around at all the wonder around us, it is hard to imagine that we are the very best, the crown jewel, the tippy top of all He has created. The wonders of His hands from the Grand Canyon to the Giant Sequoias to the Northern Lights and as unique and wonderful all His creatures, He says we are the Crown of All. We are the ones He sent His son who willingly laid down His life for us. This is mind boggling that the God of all Creation, this Holy God delights in me, in us. He sees us in our fallible and failing state as His crown jewels. He values us above all other. This is the course. This is the purpose. This is the reason. The purpose, course and reason of our very lives is to be the glory of God. We are the designated recipient of the beauty He created. We are the sole inheritance of His purpose and deity. We are His desirable and beneficial gifts to one another and to Him. Don't get thrown off course by life. Remember who you are and whose you are. Troublesome times come and go but the good love of God is always. It is eternal. The gifts, the rivers of light that flow as love, joy, peace, happiness, harmony, etc. all come from living in His cascades of Light. There isn't anything deceitful nor conniving in Him. He isn't two faced nor fickle. His purpose has been clear from creation. He desires fellowship with us and delights in us. Get back on course by recognizing that while life may not be fair, God is still who He is. While circumstances of these mortal bounds may tie you down, you are not of this world. You are a crown jewel reflecting the cascades of Light from the Father so that the sparkle of your light through Him draws others. We are crowned! We are His delight. We are kings and priests. We are His anointed and His delight. Remember who you are and straighten your crown!

You're blessed when you stay on course, walking steadily on the road revealed by God.
You're blessed when you follow his directions, doing your best to find him.
That's right—you don't go off on your own; you walk straight along the road he set.
You, God, prescribed the right way to live; now you expect us to live it.
Oh, that my steps might be steady, keeping to the course you set; Then I'd never have any regrets
in comparing my life with your counsel. I thank you for speaking straight from your heart;
I learn the pattern of your righteous ways. I'm going to do what you tell me to do;
don't ever walk off and leave me. - Psalms 119:1-8

How are we supposed to follow life's prescription given to us in Psalms 119:2?

How can we apply the principles of these scriptures in our daily lives?

Key thought for today:

Life's Prescription!

As we played the game, Blink, I could see her frustration mounting. Not because she was losing but because she was lost. She didn't understand the pattern of the game and training isn't like teaching where you stop and take the teachable moment but it is forcing the brain to find the pattern. Then it clicked, like a lightbulb suddenly turning on and her speed accelerated as the smile and confidence blossomed. She now knew how. The processing speed was increasing and her abilities with it. Soon she was on the winning track and I had to work harder to keep up. She had found the course, the pattern and was steadily gaining because she had followed the path and pattern of pace I had set. David echoes this sentiment in Psalms 119. The path of blessings, life's prescription, is to walk steadily in the road revealed by God following His directives even when they seem murky and unclear due to life's circumstances. We don't go off into our own ways but we continue to seek Him in the troubled times knowing that sticking to His roadmap is the best way. This is the life of no regrets. Staying the course under His guidance, playing the hand dealt even while not understanding its purpose. His ways are clearly not ours but they are the right ones. When we study His actions, reactions and patterns laid out so well in scripture then we begin to see His patterns and can walk more confidently and assuredly gaining the edge of peace in the knowing of who He is. Keep looking and learning His patterns and rhythms as they are without fail. If you feel lost and uncertain, keep seeking Him and following His word-the roadmap, because despite the twists and turns, the beauty that seems to be lost will be revealed. Just like a stained glass masterpiece made from the broken pieces of life, staying the course despite the trials results in beauty from the ashes. Learn the pattern of His righteous ways and stay the course because just around the next turn is the beautiful thing you have been hoping for and dreaming of forever. A prescription takes time to take effect. His prescription for life is the right way to live. Stay the course.

Don't brashly announce what you're going to do tomorrow; you don't know the first thing about tomorrow. Don't call attention to yourself; let others do that for you. The purity of silver and gold is tested by putting them in the fire; The purity of human hearts is tested by giving them a little fame. - Proverbs 27:1-2, 21

Why do we allow people and things of this world to determine our value?

How do we allow Him to determine our value and just be who He wants you to be?

Key thought for today:

Purity Test!

A test comes after the process of the teaching to see if mastery of the concepts has occurred. Another type of testing is diagnostic to see what a problem is or the cause of a set of symptoms such as in medicine or health care. Lately, I have had a lot of both physically, emotionally and spiritually. Test anxiety or worry comes from the anticipation of a negative outcome from either type of test and it is a peace stealer. I work with lots of folks who struggle with test anxiety, tension, worry and as a result carry the burdens of anxiety, panic attacks, mind shame and depression. The purity test is all about discovering who is truly in you. It is about pushing aside the anxiety of what will be, could be, might be in place of the Who is. We have a tendency to think we understand tomorrow and what will happen such that it causes a fear of failure or disappointment before we even begin. God isn't about fear nor failure. He isn't about gaining fame nor fortune. He isn't about worrying or fretting. He is the Prince of Peace. This rose is called the Peace Rose because it represents a beauty and fragrance that is uncanny but as a bud, this rose looks unremarkable and not like anything special at all. It is simply a rosebud like any other. The purity of this rose is only revealed as it blooms and opens. The unmatched fragrance and colorations are like no other and this rose is one of the most resilient flowers I have ever seen. It isn't about whether it has a certain color or not because each bud is unique in that as the flower opens, the coloration is unique to that flower and only that one. Silver and gold are precious minerals worth a lot of money but the value is raised by the purity. The fire or trials of the metals determines the purity and only by the testing of them can purity be determined. You see, like our lives, the purity tests take time and processes, heat and pressure, trials and situations. Our weaknesses only become strengths when they are made perfect through Him. The beauty of the rose isn't revealed as a bloom but only as it blooms. The purity of the metal isn't easy to tell until it is tested. Our tomorrows are not destined to be until we learn to rest in the process of trusting. The purity test of a human heart is fame and attention. The attention, draft or prediction of tomorrow only applies when we step outside Who He is. Stop being so blind and stop believing everything that people say about you. Instead allow God to be the Who and you be the unknown beauty, fragrant and pure because of Him. Quit trying to push your way, your agenda and just be His. I read a story about value and how the value of a bottle of water changes based on location and availability. We are tapped into The Source. If we allow Him to determine our value, our location, our success and our situations without trying to get ahead of who He is, the purity test will reveal this Prince of Peace with us as we walk through the trials. It will bring our beauty and fragrance out to others as we open up to Him and for Him. It will allow our purity to stand the test of fame and fortune to be Who He wants us to be-highest in value of all the precious commodities of Earth and eternity. Quit allowing the desire for fame and fortune to ruin the tomorrows He has designed for us. Just trust in Who He Is and let the rest stand the test for He is the Master of all the Materials of life. Rest in Him and bloom naturally, unfolding the purity in His Sonshine.

Now God has us where he wants us, with all the time in this world and the next to shower grace and kindness upon us in Christ Jesus. Saving is all his idea, and all his work. All we do is trust him enough to let him do it. It's God's gift from start to finish! We don't play the major role. If we did, we'd probably go around bragging that we'd done the whole thing! No, we neither make nor save ourselves. God does both the making and saving. He creates each of us by Christ Jesus to join him in the work he does, the good work he has gotten ready for us to do, work we had better be doing. - Ephesians 2:7-10

Why is it so hard to trust God through the journey of life when it is foggy and unclear?

How does understanding God's mercy and love shape your perspective on your own salvation journey?

Key thought for today:

Clear Purpose!

The fog was so thick that nothing around us could be seen. The roadway in front of us was quickly filling with traffic slowing down unsure of how to move forward because the bridge was narrow and notorious for wrecks. My husband had navigated that bridge so much in his career and traveled through fog so much that he drove it confidently and nonchalantly as I quaked inside. It didn't faze him because he knew the path, the purpose of the trip and he was anticipating good things ahead. Having vision and purpose is important to any group, organization or business but it is also important for individuals to understand where that vision or purpose comes from and to trust the person casting or driving through the fog. God has us where He wants us and He has cast His vision and purpose to us in His word. All we have to do is trust Him with His wonderfully amazing gift of salvation. We don't have a major role in the making and saving of others but we do have purpose and vision in the leading and trusting. Just as I only had the purpose of sitting in the truck trusting my husband to navigate the fog and get us to our goal when I couldn't see. It would've been easy to question him constantly and second guess his abilities and nag, advise and direct from my seat, as I often try to do to God, but the truth is that the peace came in the knowledge that I knew he knew what he was doing. I trust my husband's skills. If I can trust a mortal man to navigate a foggy, cluttered, hidden roadway through a city to my destination, why is it so hard for me to trust God through the journey of life when it is foggy and unclear? I know His purpose and vision is perfect. I know His timing is just right although this is often one of my biggest questioning places. It's God's gift, vision, purpose and good work that I am set out to do, so why is trust so hard? The answer came as I sought His face this morning. It is because I listen to other voices too often. This undermines my trust and creates fear-the peace stealer. As I rode in that truck, I had conversations with my husband and we both had lots of questions about the procedure ahead of us but we had peace in the knowing of who He is. We may not always understand what we are going through. Wrecks may happen in our lives that make us question His divine purpose but if we will trust Him to navigate, His peace will come by trusting His vision and abilities to navigate the road ahead. It is after all, every bit of it, His creation, His idea and His timing.

I pray to God—my life a prayer— and wait for what he'll say and do.
My life's on the line before God, my Lord, waiting and watching till morning,
waiting and watching till morning. - Psalms 130:5-6

Are you listening? Take the time to tune everything out and hear His heartbeat.

How can the practice of waiting on the Lord be applied in your life on a daily basis?

Key thought for today:

Lifeline!

There was a famous game show for a while called Who Wants to Be a Millionaire and during the show, when the contestants got stuck they could phone a friend as their lifeline to get an answer or advice for something they didn't know. I am so glad that I am not waiting on someone on Earth to have all my answers. Doctors are great as are other professions but we are all practicing and learning daily as we do not know all there is to know on anything-that is why it is called "practicing medicine". When we pray to God with our life as a prayer, it is a direct lifeline to God. In the middle of the night, God awoke me and told me to listen for His heartbeat. I struggled for over an hour to tune out all the other noises from the heater to the refrigerator, the animals outside and even my own body to hear Him. The moment I truly leaned back against Him and breathed to feel His heartbeat was the most incredible and intense moment of my life. I literally felt His heart and heard His heart but for a moment and then began craving it again. It is a finite thing that we get so fixated and attention pulled in so many directions that we miss that moment. I am so in awe of that moment and the things He revealed to me which I must ponder on in my heart before sharing more but the incredible intimacy is echoed in this passage that David "a man after God's own heart" wrote. My life's on the line before God, my Lord, waiting and watching till morning...waiting and watching until That morning...That morning when He will return for us. I challenge you to take the time to tune it all out and hear His heartbeat. Prayer to God-your life a prayer-in all you do and wait for what He'll say and do. He is the lifeline you need. There is no other.

Why would you ever complain, O Jacob, or, whine, Israel, saying, "God has lost track of me. He doesn't care what happens to me"? Don't you know anything? Haven't you been listening? God doesn't come and go. God lasts. He's Creator of all you can see or imagine. He doesn't get tired out, doesn't pause to catch his breath. And he knows everything, inside and out. He energizes those who get tired, gives fresh strength to dropouts. For even young people tire and drop out, young folk in their prime stumble and fall. But those who wait upon God get fresh strength. They spread their wings and soar like eagles, They run and don't get tired, they walk and don't lag behind. - Isaiah 40:27-31

Why do we tend to run away headlong into disaster, instead of turning to Him?

Why is waiting so difficult?

What are the benefits of waiting?

Key thought for today:

Stubborn Love!

As the season changes, my mind goes towards children's stories and today I was thinking about God's stubborn love and how we are so much like The Gingerbread Boy. The story is that an older couple who had no children decided to make a gingerbread boy. The gingerbread boy didn't realize that he was made for love but instead out of fear immediately jumped out of their oven and ran away into the world that was truly only after eating him or using him first for their own purposes. The sad story ends with a sly fox lying to the boy and eating him up because he bought into the lie. All along in the story, the couple who created him ran after him declaring their love and care but he was so convinced by his own fear that he ran headlong into his demise. We as a people are such hard headed ones. In Isaiah, this prophet says, Why? Why aren't you listening? Why do you not understand that God lasts forever and is in charge of it all? Why do you think He doesn't care or has lost track of you? Stop running! Turn around and hear him calling out His love as your creator. Hear His voice and know that He is your source, your energy, your renewal and your strength. You are nothing without Him and you are running away headlong into disaster and disappointment without even listening. Quit complaining and whining. Those that wait on God soar like eagles, run without weariness and walk without giving out because their hope is in the Lord who is their maker. He's got the goods to patch the flaws and freshen the stamina. I love the song about God's stubborn love because I can just see how He keeps coming but I love more the beauty of the prodigal realization that the love didn't leave when the fear and pride and selfishness made him desert his father. The Father is right where He has always been, waiting and calling. Stop running and turn towards that voice of the Creator who loves you. He didn't create you to steal your hopes and dreams. He created you to fulfill His purpose and have your hopes and dreams made new in Him. He knows you inside and out. He never tires out. He doesn't come and go. Stop running and listen to His voice.

"Be strong. Take courage. Don't be intimidated. Don't give them a second thought because God, your God, is striding ahead of you. He's right there with you. He won't let you down; he won't leave you." - Deuteronomy 31:6

What are the commands and promises given in this scripture?

Why does the world teeter off balance when it comes to claiming the promises of God?

Key thought for today:

Second Thoughts!

The commands and promises are so thickly balanced in this passage.

Be strong!

Take Courage!

Don't be intimidated!

Don't give them a second thought!

Because....here come the promises:

God, your God is striding ahead of you.

He's right there with you.

He won't let you down.

He won't leave you.

Now, let's pair them and read them:

Be strong! God, our God is striding right here with us! Wow! That's powerfully awesome!

Take Courage because God is right here with us!

Fear has no grounds! Fear cannot stay! Fear cannot win because God is right here!

Don't be intimidated because He won't let you down! This promise means not to quit because He is bolstering and holding us up!

Don't give them a second thought because He won't leave us! We are not alone! It doesn't matter where we go or what happens! It isn't a fictional superhero, character or Santa watching for us, protecting us, it is God.

Oh, that we could truly grasp these promises and walk upright with our heads held high knowing these truths.

The world teeters off balance because they want to claim the promise without the command commitment but these are tied together. Knowing confidently that God is with us, for us, holding us, supporting and guiding us, and leading us.... all of this is a result of taking faith action in the beginning. Be strong-stand in faith. Take courage-take it, not wait on it. Take courage from the word, from His promises, from confidence in who He is. Stand firm, unintimidated by the circumstances of life because we know in whom we have believed. No second thoughts. No questioning or wondering if He is who He is. No second thoughts to the situation. No second thoughts that gives seat to doubt. No wondering if, only confident courage. Be strong.

If with heart and soul you're doing good, do you think you can be stopped? Even if you suffer for it, you're still better off. Don't give the opposition a second thought. Through thick and thin, keep your hearts at attention, in adoration before Christ, your Master. Be ready to speak up and tell anyone who asks why you're living the way you are, and always with the utmost courtesy. Keep a clear conscience before God so that when people throw mud at you, none of it will stick. They'll end up realizing that they're the ones who need a bath. It's better to suffer for doing good, if that's what God wants, than to be punished for doing bad. That's what Christ did definitively: suffered because of others' sins, the Righteous One for the unrighteous ones. He went through it all—was put to death and then made alive—to bring us to God.- 1 Peter 3:13-18

Are you doing all through Christ or are you focusing on the problem/s?

Why are we to keep our focus on Him?

Key thought for today:

Heart and Soul!

I used to play a tune on the piano titled "Heart and Soul" because it required a friend to play with you. It is a beautiful piece that is haunting in the melody echoing through the piece. In Peter, he asked if we are doing good with heart and soul, do we think we can be stopped. Lots of trials may come but they are just a part of the song. The suffering is like the sharp and flats in a piano duet. They only bring out the sweetness of the harmony in resolution and resonance. Too often we get our attention onto the problem and fail to hear the haunting beauty of the crescendo resolving. Here, we are instructed to not give opposition a second thought. Peter, the man who stepped out of the boat and quickly forgot why, tells us to keep our attention in adoration before Christ, our Master through thick and thin. He tells us to be ready to speak up and tell anyone who asks why you live the way you live and always in utmost courtesy. If suffering is the way, then we do so in patient love as Christ did for us. If people throw mud at us, we keep pushing ahead with a clear conscience knowing that nothing they say will stick if we are in alignment with Him. Keep your heart on track in harmony with His and your soul will sing a melody of love throughout the suffering. The lilt of that song echoes to me still.

It isn't this song that is my heart and soul. It is Him. He is my heart and soul. If I am doing all things through Christ, then nothing else matters. It is all about the resonance with His purpose. Through it all....

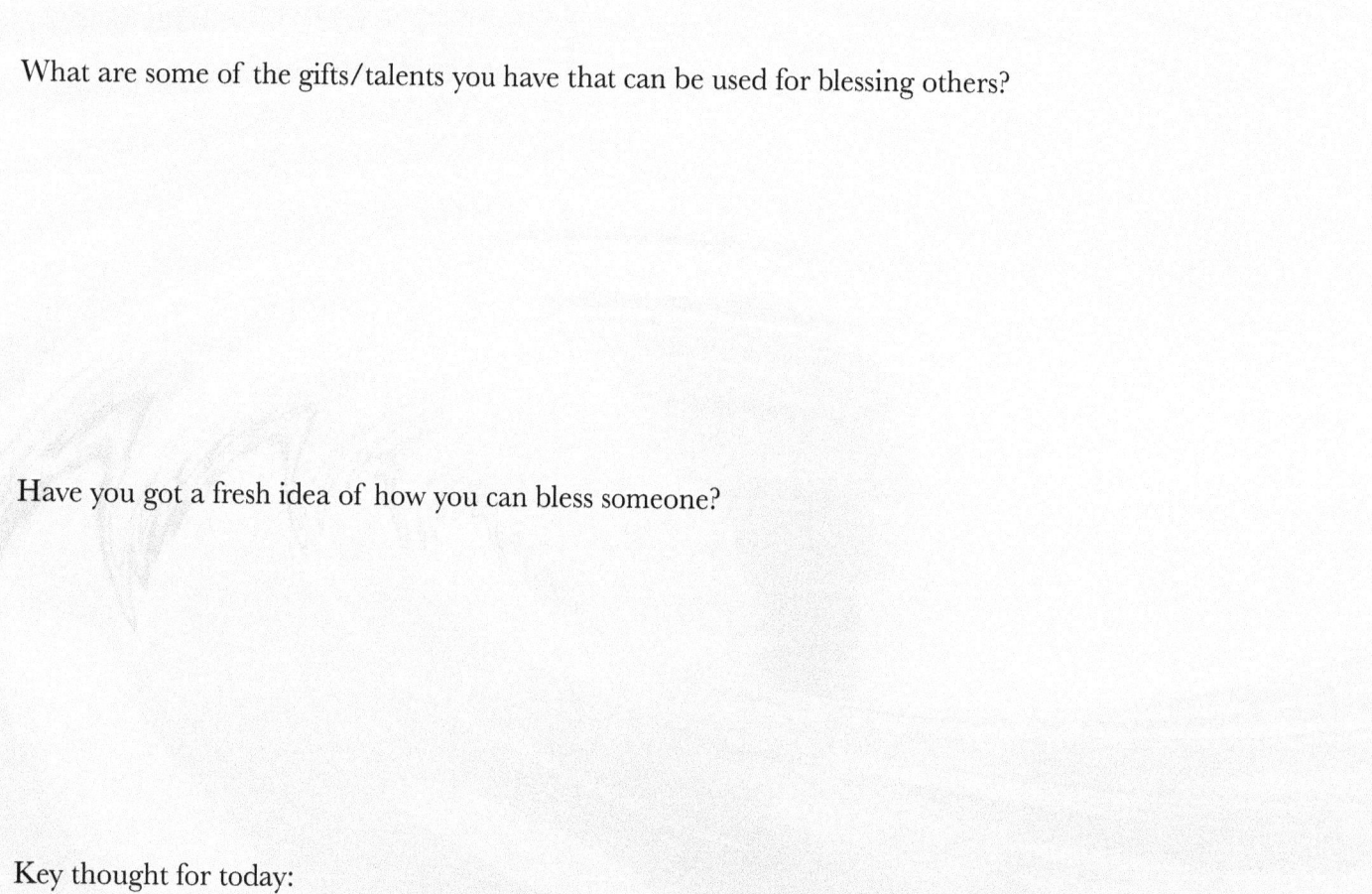

So let's do it—full of belief, confident that we're presentable inside and out. Let's keep a firm grip on the promises that keep us going. He always keeps his word. Let's see how inventive we can be in encouraging love and helping out, not avoiding worshiping together as some do but spurring each other on, especially as we see the big Day approaching. - Hebrews 10:22-25

What are some of the gifts/talents you have that can be used for blessing others?

Have you got a fresh idea of how you can bless someone?

Key thought for today:

Inventive Love!

I love creating and creative ideas. I like decorating and dreaming. I enjoy the out of the box ideas and unexpected surprises but these are things that rarely come my way. In Hebrews, we are challenged to be inventive in how we love, outreach, and spur others towards God. He tells us to keep a firm grip on the promises that keep us going as He always keeps His word. He reminds us that we're presentable inside and out through Him so we are not to waver in our confident belief but He goes on to encourage us through the words of Paul to be inventive in encouraging love and helping others out in fellowship. Recently I got to participate in a creative outreach of blessing others with gifts of beautiful jewelry. We had a book signing and a speaking event but the point was to spur each other on into reaching out to another person in our lives and beyond through a gem. Paul instructed us through the Holy Spirit that we are to be creative and inventive in spurring others around us on, in love especially now as we see the Big Day approaching. Love creatively. Live in an encouraging love life of helping others out and not avoiding worshiping together. Worship isn't only at church or in a corporate setting of believers but those connections are important to us. As the holiday season approaches each year, I ask my staff to take a blank slate of some type and creatively reimagine it. I am always fascinated by what they do with it. This year, each person was given a round piece of thin wood and told to create a door hanger of some variety. It is completely fascinating what each one did. Those who are artists at heart painted in beautiful colors and lines from themed scenes and backgrounds to create their unique pieces. Others used cards and small bits of other things like metal or wood or lights or even small village buildings to demonstrate their concepts. Each one was a labor of creativity and beauty. Each one was unique and enjoyed. The best of all was that the creativity of each person adds to the beauty of the whole. It isn't about perfection or fitting a certain mold but rather about the beauty offered in this world through each of us. Your gift of inventive love looks very different from mine but do not doubt that you have it because we are each charged by God to see how inventive we can be in encouraging love and helping out. Your talent is like no other. Your gift, your truth, your creativity is uniquely yours. Embrace your gift. Flourish in yourself to find what stretches you. Take His promises and creatively present them in a gift to another-through art, music, dance, giving, serving and loving. Let His love empower you to flow uninhibited into those around you encouraging them towards God. Plant a seed, water a flower, set up a computer, make a presentation, create a meal, develop a poem or work or art, cook a meal, serve others, etc. Go create love inventively and encourage others to come to know this God who is bigger than anything else in their lives. Let them see His loud love in you creatively and inventively. Dream and create. Love and bless. Be challenged to be all He has for you! Let's do it-full of belief and confidence in Him. After all, He is the reason for the season!

Sing to God a thanksgiving hymn, play music on your instruments to God, Who fills the sky with clouds, preparing rain for the earth, Then turning the mountains green with grass, feeding both cattle and crows. He's not impressed with horsepower; the size of our muscles means little to him. Those who fear God get God's attention; they can depend on his strength.
Psalms 147:11

What gets your attention?

Why does our perspective matter?

Key thought for today:

Attention Getting!

What gets your attention? I think this picture is a perfect example of something that is very attention getting. It shows an angel or a dove of peace, whichever you think it might be, in the night sky of northern lights. I can just see that angel singing a Thanksgiving hymn to God, who has filled the sky with light and rain, and blessed us in so many ways. Our attention is a fragile thing. So much steals our attention every day away from God and the things of God. The stark beauty of the leaves changing colors is astounding, if we take the time to look at it, but too often, we are busy running around in the traffic, in the pace of life, trying to get this, get that, be there, do that, and we miss the true beauty of His creation. Today is the day to be thankful for what we are, who we are, and the opportunities we have, even if they are things of painful perspective. Pain can be perceived as something negative, or it can be perceived as a signal that you are alive. Our perspective matters. When we look at things through the eyes of God, instead of our eyes, we perceive things differently. Whatever is bogging you down today and making you feel less than or left out or frustrated or hurting, change your perspective. Embrace it as an opportunity to be alive and be grateful and thankful to God for giving you this day.

But for right now, until that completeness, we have three things to do to lead us toward that consummation: Trust steadily in God, hope unswervingly, love extravagantly. And the best of the three is love. - 1 Corinthians 13:13

How do you define trusting steadily?

What does it mean to you to hope unswervingly?

Explain extravagant love:

Key thought for today:

The List:

Trust steadily in God!

Hope unswervingly!

Love extravagantly!

      There is something missing. We have gone to the store and yet we have forgotten something. That feeling of the missing thing we cannot put our finger on in life is frustrating and irritating but yet oh so simple to resolve. It just takes a list. My problem isn't forgetting, it is buying that extra thing I don't truly need just in case. Our spirits also walk in the need for completeness with God. It is the craving that cannot be filled without Him. The desire for more, the extra, and the intimacy. We were created to walk and talk with Him. But for right now, until the completion of His plan and His return to catch us home, we have a list that He had written for us so we would not forget. The list has three all encompassing things on it that if fully done will not only ensure completeness and intimacy but also will change our world.

Trust steadily! To be steady means to be consistent and constant. To trust means to believe with full acceptance and knowledge. If we believe with all of our heart, soul, mind and strength, consistently and with constancy, we cannot be tricked, scammed, deceived or deterred.

      Hope is an abstract word meaning to believe with faith, expectation and desire. Unswerving means to steer a straight course without distractions. If we put our whole self-heart, soul, mind, body, strength into His hands with confidence that He is steering our course and we choose to hold steady and constant through each and every bump that shakes and tries to drive us off track, we retain the eternal hope that leads to the most important element of the list: love. He doesn't just say love others. He says to love extravagantly. Extra is over and beyond. Extravagance is with nothing held back. That means that we love in fullness and through Him. Not a tainted love of man's creation. Not a sexual gratification type of love but a love full of intimacy and care that sees beyond the shallow place to the deep. Love like that is sacrificial. Love like that sees no part of self. Love like that looks only through the rose colored lenses of eternity and sees each person as Christ embodied whether they are filthy and crude or refined and wealthy. Love which is the culmination and best is the path to intimacy with Christ Jesus. We must love as He loved: completely, sacrificially and oh so deeply. Intimacy is that knowing, that completeness, that "je ne sais quoi", cannot put my finger on that perfection. This is the list that leads to the marriage consummation with the Lamb of God, Lion of Judah and Prince of Peace. His name is Wonderful, Mighty God, Everlasting Father, Alpha and Omega, Counselor, Rock of Salvation, Fortress, Defender, and so much more. Completeness is only known in the intimacy of the consummation from completing the list. Better get busy.

"Yes, I'm on my way! I'll be there soon! I'm bringing my payroll with me. I'll pay all people in full for their life's work. I'm A to Z, the First and the Final, Beginning and Conclusion. "Come!" say the Spirit and the Bride. Whoever hears, echo, "Come!" Is anyone thirsty? Come! All who will, come and drink, Drink freely of the Water of Life! I give fair warning to all who hear the words of the prophecy of this book: If you add to the words of this prophecy, God will add to your life the disasters written in this book; if you subtract from the words of the book of this prophecy, God will subtract your part from the Tree of Life and the Holy City that are written in this book. - Revelation 22:12-13, 17-19

What work or business are you about today?

Whose goals/payroll are you working towards?

Key thought for today:

Payroll!

Payday is always an interesting time. It is usually the time where people are awarded or rewarded for their labor. An award is given to recognize and honor a person's achievement, while a reward is given to someone who completes a task successfully. I love that at the end of a year, awards as well as rewards on payroll can be given. There is a lot of fraud, falseness and lies about God and who He is that abound but at the end of the day, He is the one who writes the paychecks and includes the bonus. He is the one who rewards life's work and awards a crown of life. He is the first and final, beginning and conclusion. The promise and the punishment of prophecy are clearly delineated by His word. He is on His way. He is coming soon. The payday is approaching and the hours are short to earn the wage. Scripture tells us that the wages of sin are death but the gift of God is eternal life. Even so, come quickly, Lord Jesus! What work or business are you about today? Whose payroll are you working towards? So many are so busy laying up for themselves here that they fail to see the true paycheck or pay off. Each year, I ask my employees to look ahead and set goals, cast vision, dream and plan. We do this with purpose so that we as a business can come together to grow together and become the best. God has cast a vision of a place where there is no night, sorrow or pain. God has set a timetable, a purpose, a plan and charged us to carry it forward. He has promised fulfillment, reward and said He will award a crown of life. His promises are all true. What about you? What are you doing? Whose goals are you working towards?

"If you decide for God, living a life of God-worship, it follows that you don't fuss about what's on the table at mealtimes or whether the clothes in your closet are in fashion. There is far more to your life than the food you put in your stomach, more to your outer appearance than the clothes you hang on your body. Look at the birds, free and unfettered, not tied down to a job description, careless in the care of God. And you count far more to him than birds. - Matthew 6:25-26

Do you really trust Him? Why worry or fret?

Are you spending time with Him? It's all about Him!

Key thought for today:

In His Care!

The question isn't about what we need but rather about do we trust Him. We think way too much about our clothes, food and stuff. In Matthew, Jesus says that if we decide for God that a life of God-worship isn't a life of worry and fretting but a life of freedom from the cares that life can bring. Living carefree or careless in the care of God is not about being lazy but more about taking each moment at a time. It is a little crazy to me that we fret or worry so much in this season of remembering His birth than we do any other part of the year. We worry about gifts and trees, decorations and parties, spending time with this one and that one, etc. We spend so much time fretting about these things rather than celebrating The One who came to give us freedom from worry and cares. He tells us to look at the birds of the field and see that God provides food for them just as He dresses each flower beautifully. Then He reminds us that He is jealous for us that we spend our time and focus on Him and not on other stuff. We work to provide, then we trust God to be the difference. He is enough. That is all we must do. Nothing of Earth is tied to a job description or social performance through what we wear, act or do, except what we allow. The weather is His, the timing and beauty of nature is His, the moment by moment care of everything is His and He is enough. I fret when I shouldn't and I worry about silly things like others do. I know I shouldn't so I have to remind myself often to cast my cares upon Him. I have to decide for God moment by moment. Deciding for Him means that I live a life of God worship not Me worship. It isn't all about me, it is all about Him.

This is how we know we're living steadily and deeply in him, and he in us: He's given us life from his life, from his very own Spirit. Also, we've seen for ourselves and continue to state openly that the Father sent his Son as Savior of the world. Everyone who confesses that Jesus is God's Son participates continuously in an intimate relationship with God. We know it so well, we've embraced it heart and soul, this love that comes from God. - 1 John 4:13-16

Are you constantly telling others of Him? Are you continuously embracing heart and soul all that He sends your way? Are you living in the Knowing or only the knowledge of Him? Is His life evident in you to all you meet?

How can we ensure that our love for God is genuine and demonstrated in our actions toward others?

Key thought for today:

Continuous Intimacy!

Intimacy is more than acquaintance, more than friendliness, more than spending time with someone, more than knowing some facts about them....intimacy is a level of knowledge and knowing that indicates a depth to the relationship. The Bible uses the word Know as a word of intimacy as in Adam knew Eve and they conceived a son. When the Bible indicates Know, it indicates a level of intimacy that surpasses deep knowledge and goes into a spiritual connection in relationship as well as more. In 1 John, he states The Word was God from the beginning. This is how we know we're living steadily and deeply in Him-the Knowing of Him-the Intimacy...it has a semicolon which means see what follows: He's given us life from His life, from His very own Spirit. We've seen for ourselves. We continue to state openly that the Father sent Jesus, His son as Savior of the World. This confession is the key to the Knowledge-the Knowing-the Intimacy-the Love that comes from God and invigorates heart and soul.

Intimacy comes from consistency and constancy. You can be consistent without being constant. Something is constant if it does not stop, though it may vary. Consistent things may start and stop, but do not vary. The song says....God's love is unchanging like a ring of solid gold, like a vow that is tested, like a covenant of old. His love is enduring. His love is both constant meaning it never stops and consistent meaning unchanging. God is Love-consistent and constant. I have begun lately to understand Paul's thorn in the flesh experience. As many with chronic issues or illnesses do, your mind and body get to a level of pain consistency and constancy that you learn to manage or accept as normal. You begin to live in it like an old shoe and just adapt. It changes you. It may remake the way you do things or the way you eat or any number of changes but it becomes a definitive part of your life. I see so many who go through these struggles and the struggle is real but so is the intimacy with Him. The Knowing. Not only knowing Who He is, like being acquainted but Knowing Him deeply and intimately requires Time and Effort, Consistency and Constancy. The staying and the sticking, the unchanging and unwavering faith that He is, the constant confession and testimony of who He is and always will be continues through eternity as we see in Revelation from John as he witnesses the constant and continuous worship by all in his vision. Are you constantly telling others of Him? Are you continuously embracing heart and soul all that He sends your way? Are you living in the Knowing or only the knowledge of Him? Is His life evident in you to all you meet?

So come, let us worship: bow before him, on your knees before God, who made us! Oh yes, he's our God, and we're the people he pastures, the flock he feeds. Drop everything and listen, listen as he speaks: "Don't turn a deaf ear as in the Bitter Uprising, As on the day of the Wilderness Test, when your ancestors turned and put me to the test. For forty years they watched me at work among them, as over and over they tried my patience. And I was provoked—oh, was I provoked! 'Can't they keep their minds on God for five minutes? Do they simply refuse to walk down my road?' Exasperated, I exploded, 'They'll never get where they're headed, never be able to sit down and rest.'" - Psalms 95:6-11

Where is your mind? Is it on God or yourself? Are you fighting the weeds and stickers, pushing forward through the brush instead of walking into His open path? Is your mind set on His will or your own? Are you confused by all the voices around you? Listen, He is speaking!

How do we avoid hardening our heart toward God?

Key thought for today:

Come Worship!

Exasperated at the sheer willfulness and disobedience of the ones we provide for often leads to a loss of our temperance and an explosion of anger. This is a trait that God readily admits to feeling with us. I have seen pictures of people's joke with a possum or a coyote on their seat of their car saying they had picked up a stray cat/dog and want the owner to come claim it...I have occasionally felt that way with my own kids on days that they just would not listen no matter how hard I tried. God is an infinitely patient God who has made sacrifice after sacrifice for us, yet too often, we are too willful or stubborn to acknowledge what He is trying to do. I remember one particular incident when I had gone to great lengths to do something special for someone in my life but no matter how much I tried to guide them carefully into understanding that, they were so set on their own ways that they struck out at me missing out on the wonder of what I had done first for them. My heart was broken, not only for me and my efforts as I spent lots of time, effort, sacrifice and money to provide this amazing opportunity but also for them because they missed out on a wonderful life changing experience that would have opened doors beyond their wildest imaginations. I thought then how God feels when He has paved a road for us, made a way where there seemed no way but we refuse to look at His way because our mind is set on our own way. He questions, "Do they simply refuse to walk down my road?" He has promised and provided but we are so distracted by what we want that we refuse to see and hear what He has proposed, promised and provided. It is like a clear path cut before us, made clean and clear, rocks removed, decluttered, brush removed and all we must do is walk in but we are so set on going a different direction that we are stumbling towards the thorny woods that are tearing and pulling at us because we think we see something we want and we do not trust the clear direction He has provided. The psalmist tells us to drop everything and listen as He speaks. He has provided a way where there seems no way but we must listen. Turning a deaf ear gets us into the same position as those who failed to pass the Wilderness Test. They had a clear, beautiful opportunity right before them but they let fear and a mindset of "I know best" keep them from fully experiencing what God had for them. Where is your mind? Is it on God or yourself? Are you fighting the weeds and stickers, pushing forward through the brush instead of walking into His open path? Is your mind set on His will or your own? Are you confused by all the voices around you? Drop everything and listen to His voice. Get on your knees before Him and worship. Don't refuse Him and be cursed with the "wandering spirit of never resting or being content". Just focus on Him. Find your peace in Him. Walk down His road to the place of rest. Sit down with Him and fellowship. Listen, He is speaking!

"The person who knows my commandments and keeps them, that's who loves me. And the person who loves me will be loved by my Father, and I will love him and make myself plain to him." - John 14:21

Are you fully demonstrating His love to all those around you?

How does keeping Jesus' commandments demonstrate love for Him?

Key thought for today:

Made Plain!

There was a book I read when I was growing up called "Sarah, Plain and Tall". As a youngster in high school who often felt that way next to a younger sister who was beautiful and always picked for beauty queen and homecoming court, etc., this book spoke to me that beauty was about who you were not what you looked like. My first year of teaching this book came out as a movie which was so wonderful and I still to this day love the book and movie. They spoke of a lovely person who was loved because of her love for others-her servant's heart. In John, Jesus says this clearly that the person who loves will be loved by the Father and by Jesus. But He goes before by describing that love is demonstrated by the person who knows and keeps His commandments. There is a lot of confusion in the religious world about "His commandments". Some say it is the ten given to Moses, others say those were law and Jesus fulfilled the law so the only commandments He gave are the two to Love God and your neighbor as yourself. John 14:21 says it all. Jesus says I will love him and make myself plain to him. You don't have to jump through hoops, perform certain rituals, nor do you have any religious requirements to love. God is love. Jesus gave us the primary directive which is to know God first God is love. He told us in John 4:7 that everyone who loves is born of God. He that loves God, knows God and loves others. Here is my thought, if you do everything out of love, through love, with love, then you are walking out the love of the Father which has been made plain through the Son. There is nothing more beautiful, more Godly, more valuable in life than love. I am clearly not talking about a warped definition of sexual gratification. I am talking about the sincere love that meets a person where they are and demonstrates His love to another whether that is in a hospital, on the side of a road, in an office or wherever you are today. God's love is plain, unfettered and beautiful. It is clear to those around you as a light in a dark night. Love came as a baby in a manger to a virgin on a cold, dark night and it was made plain by God that His love isn't a respecter of persons but simple, beautiful and plain so all can see. He came that we might have life. That is the Love. His love is deep, wide, clear to others and simple. It is made plain because it isn't complicated. Just love like Jesus does and He will become plain to you-beautiful, simple and lovely. You don't need to feel like you must strive to be the best, the smartest, the most beautiful nor the most talented. You are amazing like you are because He created you and your simple beauty is evident when you love. He created you just as you are. He has said you are all those things to Him. Your beauty, talents, wonders, smarts, etc. are all plain to all around you when you love with His love. Just love Him and allow Him to light you and make it plain to all that you are the Cinderella He has chosen. He is the King of Glory and you are His chosen when you choose Him. That's as plain as it gets. No complications. Just plain and simple: love like Jesus loves.

Let the peace of Christ keep you in tune with each other, in step with each other. None of this going off and doing your own thing. And cultivate thankfulness. Let the Word of Christ—the Message—have the run of the house. Give it plenty of room in your lives. Instruct and direct one another using good common sense. And sing, sing your hearts out to God! Let every detail in your lives—words, actions, whatever—be done in the name of the Master, Jesus, thanking God the Father every step of the way. - Colossians 3:15-17

Are you fully using and understanding the recipe given?

Want peace? Try being thankful for what you have instead of whining.

Key thought for today:

House of Peace!

Everyone says they want peace in their homes, families and lives and God gave us the gift of peace. He also instructed us on how to use it in our lives. The instructions are laid out like a recipe. But like a recipe, if it sits in the book or one the shelf, in the phone or is used incidentally or incorrectly, it doesn't have automatic recall and action. For peace to reign in your home, it must be the pattern of the home, the essence, the fragrance and the sense. It doesn't come from fighting, bickering, complaining nor whining . The scripture says LET as in, it is there but you must activate it. Like yeast in a package, it cannot be activated without the right conditions of warmth and living water.

Recipe for Peace in your Home: starts with LET or Allowing Him to Have Control.

Let the Peace of Christ Keep You:

In tune with each other-this means you must take time to listen and truly hear what the other person is saying

In step with each other-this means you must walk in their shoes too, not only seeing your side

In sync with each other-this means you must take time to sync up in thoughts and mindset through good communication

In togetherness-this means you must spend quality time together outside doing your own thing

Let the Word of Christ-The Message:

Have the run of the house-this means that His word should trump yours every time!

Have plenty of room in your lives-this means that you should liberally and consistently quote it, recall it, meditate on His word-walk it out, post it on your walls, on your heart, on your mirror, wherever you need it to grow...
Give you wisdom to Instruct each other-instructions to one another should only be given in Godly consideration and like me, you need to think a lot and pray a lot before you give them to make sure they are from Him and not you!

Direct one another using Good common sense-this one is tough because if you don't apply the previous things, then you will not have permission to speak into others' lives. You will overstep and get out of sync.

Sing your hearts out to God-my grandmother had this right. I never went to her house that she didn't have a song on her lips and I will always cherish that memory. She hummed and sang constantly with a song in her heart. I want to be like that.

Let Every detail in your lives be done in the Name of Jesus. If you keep the focus of Him always forefront, then the big things will work themselves out. Peace is in the knowing.

Thank the Father every step of the Way. This is the recipe to have peace overflowing as it builds confidence in who He is. An attitude of gratitude actually rewires our brain in the emotional center. Being grateful makes you a more positive person. Want peace? Try being thankful for what you have instead of whining.

Get busy not only decorating your home but creating a recipe of peace that scents your home so when others walk in, they feel it. It is your choice to activate it. The Living Water with the Right Ingredients Leads to the Bread of Life.

"Let me give you a new command: Love one another. In the same way I loved you, you love one another. This is how everyone will recognize that you are my disciples— when they see the love you have for each other." - John 13:34-35

Are you loving His way, learning to walk in His shadow, His Sonshine, reflecting His glory?

What does it look like to love the way Jesus loved?

Key thought for today:

The Love Command!

What does love look like? Everyone has a different definition. For some it is hard to define but the truth is love is as easy as the extra step, a call, a conversation, a meal, blowing leaves from their yard, listening and paying attention, etc. This command that Jesus gave was given at the last supper. He gave this command just before He walked it out: Love one another in the same way I love you. Love isn't defined in the same way to others. For some love is an action, for others it is kind words or giving...several authors have written books on love languages and how to demonstrate love yet the author of Love itself defined it best in His book. He said Love the way He loves. Love is God. To love, you must learn to walk in His shadow, His Sonshine, reflecting His glory and not yours. You are recognized by how you act and talk. Jesus says everyone will recognize you by His love walking around in you. Show His love. Doesn't matter about your opinion, it matters about His love. You cannot say I love you then never practice it or it will not be believed just like you cannot do things for others and never say the words to express love lest it not be recognized as God's love. God's love lives in you. It walks around in your life. When situations occur, remember to walk in love first and foremost-His love, not that as defined by the world. Love is His name.

So reach out and welcome one another to God's glory. Jesus did it; now you do it! Jesus, staying true to God's purposes, reached out in a special way to the Jewish insiders so that the old ancestral promises would come true for them. As a result, the non-Jewish outsiders have been able to experience mercy and to show appreciation to God. Just think of all the Scriptures that will come true in what we do! For instance: Then I'll join outsiders in a hymn-sing; I'll sing to your name! And this one: Outsiders and insiders, rejoice together! And again: People of all nations, celebrate God! All colors and races, give hearty praise! And Isaiah's word: There's the root of our ancestor Jesse, breaking through the earth and growing tree tall, Tall enough for everyone everywhere to see and take hope! Oh! May the God of green hope fill you up with joy, fill you up with peace, so that your believing lives, filled with the life-giving energy of the Holy Spirit, will brim over with hope! - Romans 15:7-13

How do we live our life so that it encourages others when they are around us?

What steps can you take to maintain a full cup?

Key thought for today:

Promises Fulfilled!

Yesterday I attended a surprise birthday party for someone turning 70. What a beautiful thing that is! Seven decades of promise fulfilled in a life full of richness. As I listened to the wisdom spoken over her life by others, I realized that we are all promises fulfilled. This picture of the Nativity behind the scripture is a testament of promises fulfilled for thousands of years. Jesus met and fulfilled promises spoken by prophets for many years and was much anticipated yet many were quick to decry Him to the point that He was crucified on a cross fulfilling yet again promises made in prophecy. Everyone everywhere can see Him and take hope! Paul says, "May the God of hope fill you with joy, fill you up with peace, so that your believing lives be filled with the life-giving energy of the Holy Spirit and brim over with Hope." Hope is the one thing that sustains life through it all. The loss of hope is the number one cause of suicide. The loss of hope should never happen because the God of Hope resides in us. It is our responsibility to stay filled to the brim and overflowing to others with hope so that those living in darkness can see the light. Light is the promise fulfilled on the darkest of nights. When Jesus was born, God put a star of hope in the sky to guide others to see Him. The star didn't go out. The hope didn't leave. Jesus was the promise fulfilled. The issue was that people quit looking and filling, instead of staying under the promise of hope, they allowed their circumstances to steal their promise. What a sad commentary! The hope was there just like the star is there. The clouds may obscure it, life may spin and try to throw it off course but it remains rooted in promises fulfilled.

Do not let life steal your joy, rob you of peace or hide your hope. Rejoice! Celebrate God in your situation and know that no matter what, there is Hope so Hold on! Look up, see His promises fulfilled through the generations and get back under the flow of the Living Water until you are filled to overflowing with His love and life. I heard a story of a cup that spilled when it was accidentally bumped. The cup spilled over onto those around it all the contents that was in it. If your life is filled with love and you get bumped by life, you will still spill out love. If your life is filled with hope and joy, then the accidents of life and the situations of uh-oh, will still spill out hope and joy. It is all about what you are filled with. Feeling down, lost, depressed, discouraged? This just means you emptied out into life and need to refill with The Living Water of Hope, Joy and Peace to the brim so when life bumps you, you will spill over onto others what He has fulfilled in your soul. Promises fulfilled are there for our sake. We cannot see the stars unless we are looking up. We cannot have hope unless we are looking to the true source of Hope-the Eternal Hope.

Blessed be God— he heard me praying.
He proved he's on my side; I've thrown my lot in with him.
Now I'm jumping for joy, and shouting and singing my thanks to him. - Psalms 28:6-7

What is a lot? A portion? A piece? A life? A chance? Will?

How can we cultivate a heart of praise amidst our trials?

Key thought for today:

My Lot!

What is a lot? A portion? A piece? A life? A chance? Will? Blessed be God because He heard me praying. The psalmist is shouting for joy and singing thanks not because he threw his lot in with God but because God proved Himself again to be on his side. Often when we get down, discouraged or upset, we forget this. God is in the proving business. He's a great God and He is on our side whether we see the answer and proof or not.

Applause, everyone. Bravo, bravissimo! Shout God-songs at the top of your lungs! God Most High is stunning, astride land and ocean. He crushes hostile people, puts nations at our feet. He set us at the head of the line, prize-winning Jacob, his favorite. Loud cheers as God climbs the mountain, a ram's horn blast at the summit. Sing songs to God, sing out! Sing to our King, sing praise! He's Lord over earth, so sing your best songs to God. God is Lord of godless nations— sovereign, he's King of the mountain. Princes from all over are gathered, people of Abraham's God. The powers of earth are God's— he soars over all.- Psalms 47:1-9

When was the last time you truly screamed a Hallelujah?

Wanna get over the blues, conquer the illness, change your worries into triumphs...What are some ways you can start with "Raising a Hallelujah"?

Key thought for today:

The Summit!

We cheer at games, fireworks, holidays and events but how often have we cheered God? I had a pastor a while back who always said "Go, God" and I loved it and adopted it because the truth is we don't cheer God enough. We have become stoic or set in how we see God in His place rather than in our everyday lives. Here's a challenge: go scream and shout to God in praise rather than in anger or complaining. I unfortunately often hear curses and slang with God's names being commonly used in frustration and hollered out in anger but I rarely hear people singing and praising in public. What would our world look like if we chose to change this? We have relegated Jesus to a baby in a manger or a crushed man on a cross who lives on two days a year-Christmas and Easter. We forget that that baby is the Savior of the World. We fail to realize that this wave walking, miracle talking Jesus is still alive and present in our world. In our day to day, we say our prayers before we eat and as we go to sleep but when is the last time you truly cheered God for the small provisions each day-the sunrise, the getting out of bed, the ability to hear, see, speak, write, taste, smell? When was the last time you truly screamed a Hallelujah? We ponder on the way this world is turning and why the church has grown old and cold but when is the last time we took time to cheer God instead of the band performing or the children's program? I remember the days of applause and cheers to God happening in church. I grew up like that. I was raised to understand that God deserves our highest praise-offering applause and praise but seriously, I have never heard the level of praise for the God of the Universe that I have heard for a movie star or even a Christian performer at a concert. When is the last time that you truly shouted God's praise? I bet you did it alone in your house or your backyard because you thought someone would think you nuts if you did it in public. That's what's wrong with this world. We have allowed the power of praise to be relegated to the weird or unstable rather than being commonplace. David is shouting God's praises here in this Psalm-here's a starting place to the summit. Wanna get over the blues, conquer the illness, change your worries into triumphs...start with Raising a Hallelujah! Again and again! Read this psalm aloud and insert your name for Jacob....He set us at the head of the line, prize winning, His favorite. Loud cheers as God climbs the summit of your life! Sing it out! Shout it out! The Lord is so good! Make His praise glorious and loud! He's King of the Mountains! Whatever your mountain is-He still reigns-He soars over all! If you are done, start praising louder in the presence of the impossible and watch the tide change!

Thank God! Call out his Name! Tell the whole world who he is and what he's done! Sing to him! Play songs for him! Broadcast all his wonders! Revel in his holy Name, God-seekers, be jubilant! Study God and his strength, seek his presence day and night; Remember all the wonders he performed, the miracles and judgments that came out of his mouth. Seed of Israel his servant! Children of Jacob, his first choice! He is God, our God; wherever you go you come on his judgments and decisions. He keeps his commitments across thousands of generations, the covenant he commanded, The same one he made with Abraham, the very one he swore to Isaac; He posted it in big block letters to Jacob, this eternal covenant with Israel: "I give you the land of Canaan, this is your inheritance; Even though you're not much to look at, a few straggling strangers." - 1 Chronicles 16:8-19

Have you claimed your inheritance from the Lord? Do you know Him?

Summarize in your own words the 10 different dynamics of claiming your inheritance from the Lord.

Why is it so important to seek Him?

Key thought for today:

Claiming Inheritance!

The conversation of inheritance has been a topic I hear a lot about as I age and work with those who are aging or passing on things to family. The inheritance from God is better than anything anyone could ever leave to us here.
How is inheritance claiming done? It is simple and spelled out here in Chronicles-the dynastic book of kings.

1. Thank God! Call out His Name! Identify yourself as His by Name! I belong to the God of the Universe! The King of Kings and Lord of Lords! I am His and He is mine!

2. Tell the Whole World Who He is and What He's Done for you. Testify to all the things He has done for you! The small and least matter as much as the greatest. You can see. You can hear. You can talk. You can walk. Recognize these blessings.

3. Sing to Him! Play songs for Him! Don't make the music about Him but for Him! Get the I, me, my out of it and move into the worship of Him!

4. Broadcast His wonders! Revel in His Holy Name! Advertising is essential to being identified as His! Let others know all His goodness and what He has done, is doing and will do!

5. Be Jubilant! Joy comes from fellowship with Him. Jubilance comes from extreme happiness in Him. Quit letting the world identify you and recognize who you are and be uplifted in Him! Jubilee comes from freedom in Him!

6. Study God and His strengths! Know Him! Read, study, spend time and energy to learn of Him and who He is!

7. Seek His presence day and night! The most important one in my opinion that sums up all. Seek Him first He says if you seek Him with all your heart, soul, mind and strength, He will be found!

8. Remember all the wonders He performed-the miracles and judgments that came from His mouth! Don't let your days get clouded by the now...remember the when and that He will do it again!

9. Recognize that wherever you are, you come under His judgment and decisions. His authority is like no other. Understand and embrace that His authority cannot be replaced by any other. His is ultimate!

10. Recognize that He keeps His covenants and commitments across thousands of generations. Look at what He has done to fulfill His covenants and recognize that His promises are true to all who seek Him.

Inheritance comes through the bloodlines or the written will. When Jesus' blood was shed for you and you accept it, He writes your name on the document of inheritance! You are chosen to receive all He has promised. Claim your inheritance by coming to know Him and accept who He is!

On your feet now—applaud God! Bring a gift of laughter, sing yourselves into his presence. Know this: God is God, and God, God. He made us; we didn't make him. We're his people, his well-tended sheep. Enter with the password: "Thank you!" Make yourselves at home, talking praise. Thank him. Worship him. For God is sheer beauty, all-generous in love, loyal always and ever. - Psalms 100:1-5

Is He your focus/theme? Make it a song of praise to Him

How do we cultivate a heart of worship, even when we are facing struggles in our life?

Key thought for today:.

The Theme!

My kids are coming home to visit and I am so excited that I plan and look forward to it. I have a thing about themes and focus-like a vision perspective and this year mine is finding the joy through the struggles. This is also the way to victory through the storms. The psalmist wrote to us in explicit directions to this theme of praise.

1. Applaud God
2. Bring a Gift of Laughter
3. Sing yourselves into His presence
4. Know that God is God
5. Know that He made us and we didn't make Him.
6. Enter with the password: thank you!
7. Make yourselves at home in Him!
8. Talk praise
9. Thank Him
10. Worship Him!

The theme is God is sheer beauty, all generous in love, loyal always and ever.
No matter what! No matter who! No matter when! No matter...He is the theme...the Why... the purpose! Get up! Get on your feet...start worshiping! Apply the formula and see if your spirit doesn't lift out of the struggle into the beauty of His love!

God spoke again to Ahaz. This time he said, "Ask for a sign from your God. Ask anything. Be extravagant. Ask for the moon!" But Ahaz said, "I'd never do that. I'd never make demands like that on God!"
So Isaiah told him, "Then listen to this, government of David! It's bad enough that you make people tired with your pious, timid hypocrisies, but now you're making God tired. So the Master is going to give you a sign anyway. Watch for this: A girl who is presently a virgin will get pregnant. She'll bear a son and name him Immanuel (God-With-Us). By the time the child is twelve years old, able to make moral decisions, the threat of war will be over. Relax, those two kings that have you so worried will be out of the picture. But also be warned: God will bring on you and your people and your government a judgment worse than anything since the time the kingdom split, when Ephraim left Judah. The king of Assyria is coming!" - Isaiah 7:10-17

What was making God tired with Ahaz?

How often do we act the same way?

Key thought for today:

God Tired?

I always heard that God never gets tired so I was surprised when I read this scripture in multiple versions of the prophet Isaiah referencing the tiredness or weariness of God towards His people. It makes sense as we are made in His image but of what is God tired? It is fatigue with the incessant selfishness of man- the pious, fake, timid hypocrisies of man. Isaiah declares the birth of Jesus right after saying God was getting tired of man's selfish ways. But I had to back up to see the rest of the story. You see, God had just once again performed an unacknowledged miracle for these people. He spoke to Ahaz and said, "ask for a sign from your God. Ask anything, be extravagant. Ask for the moon!" But Ahaz in his own mind that refuses to see the God who is, missed the mark again. So God speaks through Isaiah proclaiming the birth of Jesus and the judgment of the people in one fell swoop. God is weary of ungrateful and unappreciative people. He is tired of the wants and demands, desires for things and wealth. This creature of creation that He created for the sole purpose of fellowship with Him has left the purpose and is in constant demand for entertainment and more, more, more. God is about to deliver the coup d'état. The end of the world is swiftly approaching and yet as we spin away in the season created to celebrate His birth, we hasten to the party, the present, the tree and the performance forgetting all about who He is. Judgment is coming! Jesus is coming! The truth is ripe for harvest. God is tired. The first time God got tired of men's ways, He sent a flood. The second time, He sent a Savior. This time He sends a Warrior, a fire, a flame that burns eternally to burn away the hypocrisy and falseness this generation has constructed. Malachi says, "You make God tired with all your talk. "How do we tire him out?" you ask. By saying, "God loves sinners and sin alike. God loves all." And also by saying, "Judgment? God's too nice to judge." Malachi 2:17

It is time for repentance. Judgment is on its way.

Run, run as fast as you can...you can't catch me...says the gingerbread man...yet he was caught in his own folly. He ran from the creator into the arms of the deceiver and all was lost. Ask for a Sign from God. He sends them daily. Look to the skies. The Heavens declare Him. The Earth shudders in birth pangs. Jesus is coming soon!

For unto us a Child is born, Unto us a Son is given;
And the government will be upon His shoulder. And His name will be called
Wonderful, Counselor, Mighty God, - Isaiah 9:6

Can you describe what His name means to you?

Wonderful Counselor:

Mighty God:

Everlasting Father:

Prince of Peace:

Key thought for today:

No Substitutions!

His name is Jesus, His abilities immense, His skills are unmatched, and His government is on His shoulders but He cannot be substituted. You cannot buy, supplant, change or substitute who He is. He is more than Wonderful.

As I placed an order online to be delivered to a friend/colleague who isn't feeling well, I was asked consistently to substitute and it started getting irritating that the items I needed and wanted were not readily available then I started just being grateful that they would deliver and moved on but the constant thought stayed; for some things there is just no substitute. He cannot be substituted by any other. He is one of mind, one of a kind. He is supreme and above all. I am so glad that God saw fit to send the ultimate Lamb of God to fulfill the covenant with a once and for all sacrifice and so glad He was willing to take it all for me! No substitutes!

At once the angel was joined by a huge angelic choir singing God's praises: Glory to God in the heavenly heights, Peace to all men and women on earth who please him. - Luke 2:13-14

Peace is interpreted differently from one person to the next so how do we determine a peace on Earth?

How do we maintain our place of peace with Him?

Key thought for today:

Peace to All?

Peace and Goodwill towards Earth is what it is all about right? Wrong! Peace is a concept that is much distorted by perception. I mean peace is interpreted differently from one person to the next so how do we determine a peace on Earth? We read the full phrase as it was written. Peace to all men and women on Earth who please Him. Peace isn't the absence of problems but rather the knowing of who He is and that He is in control during the process. Jesus didn't come to Earth to bring peace. He came to fulfill the law as a new covenant closing and ending the demand for continuous sacrifice of lambs for sin. He became the Lamb of God who took away the sin of the world. But He rose again as the Lion of Judah who breaks every chain. When the Angel declared His birth, they sang glory to God for this was the birth of Jesus, the Son of God in the flesh of man. Peace is a place of certainty in Him. Pleasing God is the process of doing all we were created to do. We were created in His likeness to walk with Him, talk with Him and fellowship with Him in worship and praise. He delights in us. When we realize that is our place and our purpose, then all things align as they should and we reach the place of peace. Just like any other location though, it is a place we can stay or leave and when we get out of alignment with our purpose, then we have relocated and peace seems distant while worrying takes over. Relocation of your heart into alignment with Him is possible just by finding your purpose again. Take time to relocate your heart and mind today. Establish your purpose in Him again, establish His glory in worship and find the peace that the angel declared on the day of His birth.

Then Joseph woke up. He did exactly what God's angel commanded in the dream: He married Mary. But he did not consummate the marriage until she had the baby. He named the baby Jesus. - Matthew 1:20-25

You are charged with naming Him in your life. What will you call Him? Savior? Warrior? Friend? King? Counselor? God?

What is the significance of the name "Jesus"?

Key thought for today:

The Naming!

I am fascinated by names. Likely a good thing since I have a very unusual one, but names have power because words have power and names harness the power of The Word and embrace the person. This is why many people who have experienced trauma change their names. In olden days, your surname was your profession so a carpenter would have the last name Carpenter. So just imagine with me coming across Joseph Carpenter (again I do not know what his real full name was). He's just a guy who just got married and is excited to start life only to discover that the girl he just married says she is expecting a baby and it is God's son. Not only was it highly irregular but it was crazy to consider keeping this wife as his when culture demanded he put her aside but he loved her so planned to do it quietly. Then the angel appears in his dream. He gives Joseph the respect and responsibility of the child by charging him with naming the child Jesus to fulfill prophecy. Jesus came to save, to name us His. He came as a baby and was named Jesus Immanuel-"God saves, God is with us". I do not know the names of everyone who will read this but He does. He knows your name, your heart, your dreams, your heartaches and your very heartbeat. He knows your name. You know His name. He is as close as the whisper of His name. He responds with the breathing of His name and your breath speaks His name. Jesus. Joseph had a job to raise a king as a man. He had a job to name Him as King of Kings and Lord of Lords. He had a job to care for this tiny helpless babe and name Him as the God who saves. You have a choice too. What will you name Him? His name is Alpha and Omega, Wonderful Counselor, Prince of Peace, Mighty God, Yahweh...and the names are numerous but just as Joseph was charged with naming this babe in the manger. You are charged with naming Him in your life. What will you call Him? Savior? Warrior? Friend? King? Counselor? God? The naming matters.

Fear-of-God is life itself,
a full life, and serene—no nasty surprises.
- Proverbs 19:23

How does our perspective change our outlook on problems?

How can we as believers find comfort and assurance when facing difficult times?

Key thought for today:

No Nasty Surprises!

"The fear of the Lord leads to life, And he who has it will abide in satisfaction; He will not be visited with evil."
Proverbs 19:23 NKJV

This verse challenges me today as the year 2023 was a year full of nasty surprises from fraud to business struggle to financial hardship to personal health issues then false accusations then a car wreck, on and on I could go with all the evil I experienced this year so I had to look for context to this verse. There was none. It is one verse in a series of proverbs by King Solomon. God gave him wisdom. So why then would I experience so many horrid things which I considered nasty surprises and evil but the scripture says will not happen to me. The truth is perspective. You gotta read the whole thing. Fear of God-Respect-understanding and Whole Knowledge of Who He is, that is Life itself. That is the Life that is full and serene with no evil nor nasty surprises. As in life may dish it out, but if your mind is stayed on Him, you will not perceive these things as evil or nasty surprises that God did to you but rather as a bump in the road. I can truly say they were nasty surprises and evil perpetrated by those whose hearts are not on God but I was able to walk above them in victory because I knew who He was and is. I knew that no matter what "karma" or life dishes out, God is still good and able and willing to do all I ask or think. I know who God is. At first glance, this verse says, life is perfect with God in it, which isn't true. Life isn't perfect by man's definition. Life is life. Problems will come your way no matter who you are and some of us seem to get bombarded with them but God is greater. Understand who He is and that no matter what comes your way, assurance in Him to take care of it is your peace. Someone asked me recently what my problem was, I started to list them then I closed my mouth and said I am often not acknowledged. The truth is that I am blessed to be alive. My problem is that I often get consumed with myself and have a little pity party. I fail to look at Him and instead I lose focus and start seeing only the problem instead of The Problem Solver! Problems will come. Perception makes them mountains or molehills. Look up to the hills from whence comes our help-the Lord, the Maker of Heaven and Earth. A serene life isn't a perfect one. A serene life is one with the right perspective. Bad days come and go. Bad things happen but none of these can change who He is as long as we remember where to focus. Fear of God is Life itself. It truly is a full life and serene-because those nasty surprises were expected and dealt with through Him! Do I expect problems? Sure, they are going to come. But I know that Greater is He that is in Me than he that is in this world. Son-shine time!

"You're all I want in heaven! You're all I want on earth! When my skin sags and my bones get brittle, God is rock-firm and faithful. Look! Those who left you are falling apart! Deserters, they'll never be heard from again. But I'm in the very presence of God— oh, how refreshing it is! I've made Lord God my home. God, I'm telling the world what you do!"
Psalms 73:25-28 MSG

God is rock-firm and faithful but when the first conflict happens, we dump Him quickly. Why?

What can we do to remain strong when things look impossible?

Key thought for today:

All I Want!

Song after song is written about what someone wants from "All I Want is You" to "All I Want for Christmas is My Two Front Teeth". We as humans want constantly. We want to look older, then we want to look younger. We are so consumed with what we want that we fail to live in His presence as He desires, where the blessings are. God is rock-firm and faithful but when the first conflict happens, we dump Him quickly. Why? Because if our wants are not immediately met, then we fail to want to stay in the waiting. It is in the staying and the waiting that the glory lies. When our minds get fixed on Him as all we want or desire in all of Heaven and Earth, then we begin to see things clearly. I love this picture because it looks like a boat surrounded by a rainbow but it is really a picture taken of a cloud with a rainbow around it from an airplane. It is a beautiful picture of the waiting on His promises though. You see Noah didn't just jump into the ark then all his promises came true with no problems. I am positive it was a loud and stinky place, very scary and seemed to go on forever. I know it rained 40 days and nights but it also took months for the water to recede. Then there was nothing. Starting over from scratch after a huge storm in your life is hard. Sometimes things look impossible but if you will praise Him through the storms and stay still in the waiting, He has all things worked out for your good. Just rest in Him and know. Sing this song the psalmist wrote. You, God, are all I want in Heaven and on Earth.

So let's not allow ourselves to get fatigued doing good. At the right time we will harvest a good crop if we don't give up, or quit. Right now, therefore, every time we get the chance, let us work for the benefit of all, starting with the people closest to us in the community of faith. - Galatians 6:9-10

Why do we often get fatigued in doing good?

What are some practical ways to avoid growing weary in doing good?

Key thought for today:

The Chance!

Gamblers struggle with Lady luck because of chance. Opportunities knock because of chance. Fate dictates our course. All these sayings derive from the belief that chance is something that happens to us rather than it being our choice. It wasn't by chance we were created in this time and place. It isn't by chance that we choose to do good. Chance is opportunity. Opportunity always exists. We just must embrace it as it is provided. Giving up or quitting because we get tired of trying is the only time that chance takes the lead because then it relies on others. We are cautiously warned to not stop doing good no matter what and to take every opportunity presented to work for the good of others beginning with those closest to us outwardly. Specifically Paul writes, "Let us not allow ourselves to get fatigued doing good." This is important because it indicates that it is our choice and our ability as well as responsibility to manage our fatigue. Sometimes we pour and pour and work and work then we get a Martha attitude that we are doing it all which makes us weary and tired-fatigued. When we overdo, we get an attitude towards those who do less which causes our good to become a burden rather than a joy. This is why we are told to manage it. Paul knows that if a farmer constantly and tiresomely works, he will wear out and be too fatigued for the harvest but if he manages his economy, his threshold for doing then he will thrive and see the harvest. God has promised that we will reap a good crop if we don't give up or quit. He says we must take every opportunity presented whether it be in the grocery line or in our place of business to love on others and give of ourselves, but we must manage the outflow. I have a faucet in my kitchen that requires you to quickly turn it to full volume or it will leak if only turned to a lesser flow. I think we are often like that faucet. Rather than repairing the issues in our lives, we keep going full throttle until we burn out. Our job is to manage the allotted amount of outflow so we stay full of Him. If you constantly pour but never fill, you will empty. But if you are a fountain, you will constantly flow because you are constantly refilled from the outflow in your spirit. The difference between a waterfall and a fountain is the source of fill. Jesus says He is our Living Water that never runs dry. He is our constant source. Now it is up to us to not allow fatigue while doing good-manage the flow of fill and pour. And it is up to us to get our leaky faucets fixed. If we have an area in our lives that is requiring only a full throttle without a governor, then we must put on those brakes and get it corrected. The only way to finish the race, reap the harvest and stay in joy is to stay in the overflow of His mercy.

Why would you ever complain, O Jacob, or, whine, Israel, saying, "God has lost track of me. He doesn't care what happens to me"? Don't you know anything? Haven't you been listening? God doesn't come and go. God lasts. He's Creator of all you can see or imagine. He doesn't get tired out, doesn't pause to catch his breath. And he knows everything, inside and out. He energizes those who get tired, gives fresh strength to dropouts. For even young people tire and drop out, young folk in their prime stumble and fall. But those who wait upon God get fresh strength. They spread their wings and soar like eagles, They run and don't get tired, they walk and don't lag behind. -
Isaiah 40:27-31

Why do we try to go it alone, when we have a God who is always there?

How do we cultivate a deeper trust in God's faithfulness and strength?

Key thought for today:

The Pity Party!

When you are tired, everything and everyone around you is wrong. You start feeling like a mess and the spiral of pity starts like water circling a drain. The tornadic rush of emotions becomes the focus and the complaints pile up like debris in a tornado. The psalmist understood this as he penned this song. One of my favorite songs of all time is "It is Well with my Soul" because by our standards it was not well with the songwriter's life or emotions. He had just lost his entire family to a tragedy and he penned the most tranquil and beautiful song about peace. This is because peace isn't a lack of issues or problems but despite the situations, you have a confidence expressed here by the psalmist. "Don't you know anything? Haven't you been listening? God doesn't come and go! God lasts! He is the creator of all you can see or imagine. He doesn't get tired out, doesn't pause to catch His breath and He knows everything, inside and out." The psalmist expresses the difference in us and God. We are human and foible. He is God and infinite. We fail, tire and get discouraged. He energizes us and gives us the strength to encourage ourselves and soar again. I remember watching my son fly his plane as he had to practice touch and gos. As the plane came in, you expected it to land but it would touch down, then lift again as if it was on a beam of an infallible circle. God has given us the same lift in the moment of doubt. We only need to touch earth for a moment then realize that He is still the wind beneath our wings. We soar on Him not in our own strength. If a plane relied only on the fuel and engines but never achieved lift after its thrust, it would never soar. If a bird doesn't open its wings and catch the lift, the breeze to soar, it would flap continuously and tire easily. What I am trying to say is, you cannot do it alone. It is impossible. And why try? God is there for you, ready to hold you, lift you up and be the wind beneath your wings no matter what-that is the peace, the confidence and where the true party starts. Quit having a pity party and doing the "oh me" scene, Start rejoicing in who He is and watch the lift, feel His Spirit wind begin to lift you out of the tornado debris into a place of shelter and calm. It is Well with My Soul-He's got it!

God has set his throne in heaven; he rules over us all. He's the King!
So bless God, you angels, ready and able to fly at his bidding, quick to hear and do what he says.
Bless God, all you armies of angels, alert to respond to whatever he wills. Bless God, all creatures,
wherever you are— everything and everyone made by God. And you, O my soul, bless God! -
Psalms 103:19-22

Blessing God is…

What is the key to being rich in love?

Key thought for today:

Rich in Love!

Psalms 103 is a fabulous song which is all about the richness of love in blessing God but I think we forget to bless God for His richness to us in this time of see, want, get. Everything and everyone is made by God and subject to God whether they acknowledge it or not. The truth is that He rules over us all as He is The King! But we have a choice-to bless God-to be quick to hear and do what He says and in turn we receive the richness of His love and His favor. Blessing God is being alert to respond to whatever He wills as it happens with an innate trust that He is in control. The will to do or not was given to us. I can imagine being an angel that is in His presence looking down at the simple, willful people that we are and just shaking my head that God still wants to bless us despite our selfish ways. The willful, disobedient angels were cast out of Heaven for eternity along with Lucifer. Those who stay experience His richness of glory and presence of love constantly. Those who were cast out are constantly bemoaning their bad choice and go about their evil purposes of causing havoc in this world for they know and understand the richness of love and blessings that God feels for us. They understand His favor and His goodness which they will never again experience. As one year winds down into another here on Earth, the Heavens are not impacted. The timing of the sun/moon that affects our lives so much has no impact on them. The psalmist in this song lists reason after reason for us to bless God: "He forgives your sins—every one. He heals your diseases—every one. He redeems you from hell—saves your life! He crowns you with love and mercy—a paradise crown. He wraps you in goodness—beauty eternal. He renews your youth—you're always young in his presence." Psalms 103:3-5.

He has many reasons to bless God listed in this chapter but the main one trumps them all: His richness of love. Wealth is an attribute that many strive for believing it to be a problem solver and there are many good things that money can buy but wealth cannot buy love. It may buy favor for a time but it cannot buy love. Love is a genuine gift that is far more valuable than any riches and in it resides blessings. God's love is the creme de la creme. The top of the pyramid of the best of all there is to have, possess and covet, is free to all men and women yet many do not know this or disdain this as those foolish angels who will forever regret their folly. His love is rich. His love is unfailing and full of forgiveness. His love is unconditional for the repentant and eternal. All things that come from wealth will fade away but His richness of love never will. Quit chasing the money dream and chase the richness of His love. Bless God for His goodness. Wealth and favor reside in Him. Goodness resides in Him. All we need resides in Him. Bless the Lord oh my soul...oh my soul, Bless His Holy name. As the new year approaches, choose to bless Him with all He has done for you, to you, through you and all He has prepared and provided for you. This is the key to being rich in love.

But in the end, does it really make a difference what anyone does? I've had a good look at what God has given us to do—busywork, mostly. True, God made everything beautiful in itself and in its time—but he's left us in the dark, so we can never know what God is up to, whether he's coming or going. I've decided that there's nothing better to do than go ahead and have a good time and get the most we can out of life. That's it—eat, drink, and make the most of your job. It's God's gift.-
Ecclesiastes 3:9-13

What is your vision, your word, your purpose for the next part of your life?

How do we find a balance between the temporal and the eternal?

Key thought for today:

In The End?

Ecclesiastes is a tough book to read and not for the faint of heart. King Solomon, who was given wisdom and wealth by God, had seen it all and he was downtrodden by the experience of life. He was definitely in the feels at the time. Here he had watched and experienced all that life had to offer, money, fame, love of others, etc. and he declares that there is nothing but smoke to this life and there is only one thing to do in the end: fear God.

"But regarding anything beyond this, dear friend, go easy. There's no end to the publishing of books, and constant study wears you out so you're no good for anything else. The last and final word is this: Fear God. Do what he tells you. And that's it. Eventually God will bring everything that we do out into the open and judge it according to its hidden intent, whether it's good or evil."

Ecclesiastes 12:12-14

We come to the end of a year which in my life has been profoundly tough. This year has had so many curses and challenges but it has also had so many blessings. If you look at life as the sand in an hourglass, it is nothing but running out. Each grain a day, a month or a year of life and as the years pile up, our perspective becomes less Earth focused and more eternity focused. The fireworks in the sky declaring a new year has begun only signal the turning of a day but the celebration is because men need to hope for a better tomorrow. In this portion of Ecclesiastes, Solomon understands the beauty that God creates from life but He is frustrated with the meaning of life. He has tasted all life has to offer and has seen the unfairness, the corruption, the lies and the falseness. This is the biggest argument against God that atheists have. The conclusion by this man filled with wisdom of God is that we are to live life fully, enjoy our jobs and fear God. That is all. We do not control God nor understand His ways and reasons but we do know He takes the broken and makes the beautiful. His timing is like no other. His plans far outstrip any others. Life is temporary but eternity is forever. Our role is to live life to the fullest in worship and praise to God...this is the practice ground for eternity. Our role is worship. Our job is praise. Our end is the beginning. Go ahead, have a good time and enjoy life. This is God's gift to us to enjoy Earth and celebrate Him. He walks with us and talks with us through His Spirit. Quit trying to make life into a race. It is a beautiful journey of memories. It is a celebration and a gift. Life isn't perfect but it is beautiful in all of its forms. Yes, there are a lot of smoky, unclear and frustrating things about life that we do not understand why. When things don't go our way, sometimes we doubt God but the truth is that a masterpiece fashioned in stained glass comes from broken pieces. In answer to his question in this passage, he concludes that only what we do for God lasts. So here is your task, do today for others what you would have God do for you. If you desire love, love others. If you want gifts, give. If you crave wealth, invest in His kingdom. If you desire a full life, then live each day in blessings by counting the good more than the bad. Fear God, worship God and Trust Him in all things. I'm the end, that is all that matters. What is your vision, your word, your purpose for the next part of your life? Change is going to happen so be the change. Be the difference. Enjoy and celebrate God's gift of life to you each day! He has purpose for you!

"Your eyes are windows into your body. If you open your eyes wide in wonder and belief, your body fills up with light. If you live squinty-eyed in greed and distrust, your body is a musty cellar. If you pull the blinds on your windows, what a dark life you will have!- Matthew 6:22-23

Why do we lose focus on the things that really matter?

How can our focus and perspective influence our daily lives, both physically and spiritually?

Key thought for today:

Turn Your Eyes!

Recently I got glitter in my eye from my eyeshadow and boy did it aggravate my eye. For days I couldn't focus right nor would my eye quit hurting. Worse, when I tried to see in light, it reflected, making it worse. Finally I realized I was either going to have to wash it thoroughly as just eye drops weren't working. Thankfully the washing worked, clearing my vision and the pain. In Matthew, Jesus says our eyes are windows into our body and if we open wide in wonder, our body fills with light. Meaning if we look brightly, openly and expectantly, our opportunity to have beautiful light refracted to our world is there. Quit pulling the blinds closed on the wonderful things God has for you because you are living in greed and mistrust. Wash those eyes thoroughly and get rid of the musty nastiness that has clouded your vision for far too long. Wake up to the new possibilities and opportunities that God has for you in Him. Look up and see the beauty and the light for it is there as there is always light in the darkness as He is the Light of the World.

But whoever catches a glimpse of the revealed counsel of God—the free life!—even out of the corner of his eye, and sticks with it, is no distracted scatterbrain but a man or woman of action. That person will find delight and affirmation in the action.- James 1:25

Have you caught a glimpse of who He is? Are you allowing Him to guide you in His fully revealed counsel?

How does God's word provide freedom and true liberty?

Key thought for today:

Revealed Counsel!

The free life is what every person craves and yet most are in bondage to sin without even acknowledging it. The free life is the life of revealed counsel of God and it frees the person from the rigors of the weights of public opinion. The delight and fulfillment or affirmation of life is God's gift of action. Once you catch a glimpse of who God is, you know. Following that glimpse into action is the choice of a lifetime. Many people catch a glimpse of a career they want and are willing to lay everything down for that or perhaps it is a child or a person that they turn their back on everything else to spend time with that one, but few, oh so few, actually catch the glimpse of Jesus and then fully turn their eyes on Him. The auroras fascinate me because this is what I see, a glimpse of Heaven, a brief light show of the battle waging between Heaven and Earth, a light in the shadow of the reality of the spirit world which exists yet so few acknowledge or recognize it for what it is. The revelation of God's counsel is not something man can control. It is far more than that. Last night as I walked past the wall of windows towards my backyard, I caught a glimpse of sparks and smoke. Immediately I stopped to see because fire is a dangerous thing when you live near the woods. Thankfully it was shortly followed by lots of sparkles and pops as the neighbors nearest to us were celebrating the turning of the year. Catch a glimpse of Him and follow it to His fully revealed counsel. It is worth every sacrifice and there is nothing else like it.

So let's do it—full of belief, confident that we're presentable inside and out. Let's keep a firm grip on the promises that keep us going. He always keeps his word. Let's see how inventive we can be in encouraging love and helping out, not avoiding worshiping together as some do but spurring each other on, especially as we see the big Day approaching.- Hebrews 10:22-25

What are some ways we can encourage others to stay the course?

Who or what is an encouragement to you?

Key thought for today:

Innovation!

The fad has swept social media and everyone is either showing theirs off or crying foul towards the concept. Whether it be the colors you see in a dress, changing your profile pic to a giraffe or creating an innovative cup because you do not understand people waiting hours in line to buy one, fads come and go. Scripture says there is nothing new under the sun but in Hebrews we are instructed to be inventive or innovative towards motivating others towards encouraging love and helping others out. Recently, I was asked to contribute towards a creative think tank of ideas that would encourage others to tinker with differently towards the reading and learning process. This is a passion of mine so naturally I joined but shortly discovered that what they really wanted was just creative marketing ideas for their soon to launch product not a truly out of the box approach towards reading and learning. Obviously that was not the right place for me. I want to be in the firm grip of God's promises fulfilling what He called me to do, full of belief and confidence that He is soon coming again to fulfill His promises. I see the Big Day approaching. I know that there are troubles here that fill our hearts with fear and freedoms we all hold dear are at stake. I want to stay humble before Him but spur others towards Him in creating a beautiful image of who He is for others. I read a book long ago called It Looked Like Spilt Milk. It was about how we see clouds that look like other things. It was about the power of imagination and how it motivates others. I love the aurora even though I know the science says it is just magnetism and solar flares in the atmosphere, I see it as the glimpse of the veil between our world and the spirit world. The beautiful angelic presence often depicted, the creative swirls of color and the sheer awesomeness of this fascinates my mind. I look forward to the day that the veil is dropped and the truth is seen that we are surrounded with a cloud of witnesses who see us and know us. Not just angels but our loved ones who have gone before watching and encouraging us from the sidelines of glory reveals the fullness of who God is. We are encouraged to run our race with patience, tenacity, fortitude and creativity spurring others towards the finish line. We are given the path; our training is sure; the promises and rewards await. Now it is time to get running with innovation towards that mark of the high calling. The race has begun. The cheers are ringing out from the crowd of witnesses. Don't give up or give in. Your path or mission field you are called to is uniquely yours. Your lane to run towards the prize. Give it all you have and keep pushing towards the finish line. Don't look behind in regret nor to the right or left to compare but keep pressing in towards that mark and be innovative in encouraging others towards the prize of love, worshiping together as we run, celebrating victories as we spur one another on. Stop the bellyaching whining and get a firm grip on His promises. Then let's do this-full of belief and confident in Him.

So we're not giving up. How could we! Even though on the outside it often looks like things are fall-ing apart on us, on the inside, where God is making new life, not a day goes by without his unfolding grace. These hard times are small potatoes compared to the coming good times, the lavish cele-bration prepared for us. There's far more here than meets the eye. The things we see now are here today, gone tomorrow. But the things we can't see now will last forever.- 2 Corinthians 4:16-18

Why do we become discouraged and look at things from an outward appearance only? Where should we be looking?

How can focusing on the eternal impact our lives in the present?

Key thought for today:

Small Potatoes!

Seed potatoes are small but powerful because they grow as the root of all under the ground, propagating more and more potatoes quickly. Above the ground, things kinda look like the plant is dying and not doing much but underneath on the inside, the miracle is happening. Believed to be first cultivated by the Inca Indians in Peru around 8,000 BC to 5,000 B.C, the potato is the original Superfood. For decades this nutritional powerhouse (100 calories, little fat, and an excellent source of potassium and vitamin C was one of the most reliable sources of caloric energy. They're rich in vitamin C, which is an antioxidant. Potatoes were a life-saving food source in early times because the vitamin C prevented scurvy. Another major nutrient in potatoes is potassium, an electrolyte which aids in the workings of our heart, muscles, and nervous system. Potatoes are life sustaining and long lasting but they look like nothing important at all. I have made all kinds of foods from potatoes including bread. This isn't a food lesson but a focus lesson. Often we look only at what we see and miss the true richness of the loss. When it looks like things are falling apart on the outside, the internal, unfolding grace of our Father in Heaven is working on our behalf. When things look impossible, the possibility is growing quietly. I remember the day I went to franchise training and the franchisor looked for big things from others but expected my center to be small potatoes without much activity or effect on the national stage. In fact, I asked him what he would do if I made a million dollars the first year, he flippantly said he would send me on a cruise and he did because the small potatoes can make a lot if they are invested properly into God's care. New life comes from the old giving way. This life we invest in daily is just a fad, a fading away to what life really is in His presence. It isn't what you see that matters but what you don't see. Words penned to paper become life to another because they were recorded. The ugly and unappealing places of our lives are the places where the growth happens just like the eyes of the seed potato. That nasty looking growth is a root that will soon anchor the plant and become the nutrient to nurture more growth. We often get into mental places where we doubt our purpose and plan but that is when we need to get out a potato to reflect on what it is. The outside may look like nothing, worthless and dead but the inside has life... the root of life to bring new life to our hungry bodies or to grow into new potential. You may feel like a small potato but remember whose small potato you are and go root in Him. Grow, produce and feed. The potential of tomorrow is almost here.